The Golden Link
Gospel Playlets for Parish Liturgies

By Larry Mullaly

©1985 by Resource Publications, Inc.
160 E. Virginia Street, #290
San Jose, CA 95112
All rights reserved.
ISBN 0-89390-058-3

DEDICATION
To the Children of Our Lady of Mount Carmel Parish:
our inspiration for the present,
our hope for the future.

Typography, illustrations, and cover design by Karen Dewey

Library of Congress Catalogue Card #84-60421

CONTENTS

INTRODUCTION

In the playlet entitled *The Golden Link,* a story is told of a small box containing pieces of jewelry. The various metal links were perfectly formed. But all were spiritually blind. Despite their individual beauty, they failed to see either incompleteness or the presence of other pieces lost in the shadows.

The allegorical drama of the *Golden Link* was originally intended to apply to the unborn, the handicapped, and the elderly. But it also could be related to the role of children in the formal worship of the community. Liturgy, of course, does not exclude children. Yet by and large it is assumed that worship, the celebration of Christ's Word and Sacrament, is too adult a reality to allow for contributions by the young. True, children do take leadership parts in school Mass or small group gatherings. When the full community assembles, however, the young are invariably relegated to being passive followers. They are not part of the chain which links the parish as one.

This need not be the case. The experience of Our Lady of Mount Carmel Parish in Mill Valley, California, has shown that in one area at least — that of liturgical drama — the young can become the community's "Golden Link," joining all ages and social groups in a common experience of the Good News.

The presence of short dramatic presentations within the Liturgy of the Word should come as no surprise. Drama is as old

as mankind with roots closely tied to religious ritual. Of all the
art forms, it is one of the most effective means of expressing the
wonderment of the Good News. What is remarkable is that,
when enacted by children in an honest if amateur way, a simple
dramatic presentation is often far more penetrating than the
words of the best trained lector or inspired homilist. This special
gift of the young is something shared by all our communities,
and a charisma which can readily be tapped.

The playlets presented here seek to do justice to the needs of
good liturgy, enriching the worship of the community without
overshadowing it. For this reason they are brief, doing away almost entirely with props and costumes. They are not meant to
replace either the proclamation of the Gospel text or the homily
of the priestly minister, but serve as natural bridges between
them.

The playlets which follow were written for various liturgical
occasions. The more complex presentations were initially intended for occasional evening Masses shared by our junior high
religious education students with their families. In this unhur-
ried setting, it was possible to present works such as *Martin
Who?* and *The Word of the Lord* with recorded music and slide
accompaniments. Rarely were parts memorized. With script in
hand, students would huddle beside a simulated shepherds'
campfire, or re-enact the role of pope or prodigal son. Most of
the playlets, however, were written for the principal Sunday liturgy of the parish, hosted once each month by religious education and parochial school youngsters of the same grade. In this
context, the playlets were short and keyed to the theme of the
Sunday scripture readings. Parts were memorized, although a
student prompter was always close at hand.

In both circumstances, family Mass or Sunday liturgy, it is
worthwhile to keep in mind that the playlets were written with
an adult community in mind. Children find them enjoyable and
draw much from them. But they must be explained by the homilist
to be fully effective.

The playlets give very brief notes regarding staging. Much de-
pends on the physical layout of the church and the sound sys-

tem available. In most cases, actors are grouped about one or two microphones. When an additional announcer or commentator is among the required roles, the lector's stand is also used. Scripts referring to lights are usually performed in a darkened church with illumination provided by one or two ordinary desk lamps set on the floor or affixed to chairs or step ladders.

Jesus tells us that within his Father's house there are many mansions. So too, within the modalities of worship there are many possible expressions. For some half-dozen years, the presentations given here have enriched not only those who enacted them, but our entire parish family. We are happy to share them with you.

THE GOLDEN LINK

A Playlet for Respect Life Month
(Primary Grades)

Characters: Narrator
Golden Link
Link 1
Link 2
Link 3
Link 4
Piece 1
Piece 2
Piece 3
Piece 4

Setting: Narrator reads from pulpit or microphone placed at side of acting area. LINKS 1-4 stand in a line centerstage while PIECES 1-4 sit or crouch out of sight near Communion rail.

Narrator: On the top shelf of a bedroom closet, there was once a box filled with links from an old necklace. Most of the pieces were lost in the shadows, but at the center of the box, where the light reached through, a few silver links sat and admired themselves.

Silver Links:	It's so good to be not like the others, to be bright and strong and clean. Oh look at me, I'm silver and shiny, the best I've ever seen!
Narrator:	Then one day another piece was put into the box, a golden link, far brighter and dazzling than anything they had ever seen. The silver links were so struck by the beauty of the golden link that one of them spoke out and said:
Link 1:	What *are* you, anyway?
Golden Link:	I'm a link, just like you. I want to be part of a chain. But why are you all standing alone admiring yourselves?
Link 1:	Because I'm so lovely.
Link 2:	Because I'm so perfectly formed.
Link 3:	Because I'm so strong.
Link 4:	Because I'm so shiny.
Narrator:	For a moment the golden link seemed surprised by their answers. Then it replied:
Golden link:	You may be a great bunch of *links,* but you are not much of a *chain!* Why, you cannot even stretch from *here* to *there*
Link 2:	I'm sure *I* can stretch from here to there, just watch!
Narrator:	The link stood up straight and stretched and stretched until it almost burst into tiny pieces. But it was no closer to here and there than when it had started. The link became sad and began to think only of itself.
Link 3:	Well if one of us can't do it *alone,* surely we can do it *together!*
Narrator:	So the silver links formed themselves up into a chain and stretched and stretched until they almost

burst into tiny pieces. But still they had not reached from here to there. (Brief pause) Then they *all* became discouraged. They separated, and each went back to thinking only of itself.

Link 4: Golden link, why did you come here in the first place? We were so happy. Now we are sad.

Golden Link: But you *can* reach from here to there! Look about you at all the other pieces there are.

Link 2: I don't see a thing.

Golden link: You haven't looked hard enough. Look over there! and there! and there! Come here you other links. We *need* you!!

Narrator: Lo and behold, from out of the shadows and from under the dust there appeared other links who had been there all this time unnoticed. They all came forward one by one as the golden link called them.

Piece 1: I'm old and shakey, but if there was someone to hold me, I would be strong again.

Piece 2: I have a funny shape, but if you let me hold *you,* I will never let you go.

Piece 3: I am tiny and delicate, but if you hold me, I will hold you up as well.

Piece 4: I have been broken and mended many times, but I will be happy to help.

Narrator: But as they began to form up into a chain, the silver links thought to themselves:

Link 1: No longer will I be so lovely.

Link 2: Nor so perfectly formed.

Link 3: Nor so strong.

Link 4: Nor so shiny.

Narrator: But they were *wrong.* The miracle was that not only were they able to reach from here to there, but once they had joined together, their chain emerged as a beautiful necklace. Each link was made more attractive by the pieces next to it, and the entire whole became more lovely than any of the individual pieces could ever have hoped to be. *The end.*

MARTIN WHO? THE MEANING OF A SAINT

A Playlet for All Saint's Day
or the Feast of Martin of Tours
(Junior High)

Characters: Two readers (dressed as acolytes)
The Announcer
Mrs. Bee, an elderly woman
Professor Wesser, an historian
Mr. or Ms. Flash, an advertising specialist
Mr. or Ms. Murk, a Sociographer

Setting: On the floor before the altar is an assortment of large silhouette paintings (shadow portraits which the students have made of one another). Action takes place at front-center area of sanctuary with MRS. BEE visible, sitting off to one side.

Narrator: Because the Church is a sign of God's abiding love, we say it is holy. This applies not merely to the Sacraments and its beliefs, but to its members — you and me. It applies in a special way to those whom the Church recognizes as saints, as we shall see in our playlet: "Martin Who? The Meaning of A Saint."

Readers: (In unison) Holy, Holy, Holy Lord God of Might and Power
Blessed is this man Martin, who came in the name of the Lord.

O God, by his life and death, Martin offered you worship and praise.
Renew our hearts so that we may do the same.
Saint Martin, pray for us.

Announcer: (Speaking to the audience) Members of the audience: We are gathered here this evening to modernize our collection of pictures, weeding out those which no longer have any general value. To help us do this, we have invited representatives of three distinguished professions: Professor Wesser of the University Department of History, Ms. Flash of Madison Avenue advertising, and Dr. Murk, the well known sociographer. While these pictures no longer have any use to us, we will allow our experts to claim anything which may have particular value to them.

Our first speaker will be... (The announcer stops in mid sentence, interrupted by Mrs. Bee who has walked out from altar left and begins looking through the pictures piled on the ground. With some irritation the announcer asks) Excuse me, Ma'am: what are you doing?

Mrs. Bee: I'm looking for the picture of Martin whom the Church celebrates each year on this day.

Announcer: Are you with those other two over there (he gestures to the pulpit)?

Mrs. Bee: I'm not sure: I'm just an ordinary Christian. My name is Mrs. Bee.

Announcer: Well, Mrs. Bee, that's very nice. But we do have some *very* important speakers with us whom we are waiting to hear from, and who have first claim to these old pictures. So if you'll please stay to the side for the time being.

(Mrs. Bee limps quietly off toward the pulpit and sits in clear sight with her head bowed on the altar steps. The announcer leaves his mike, picks up and displays the first picture, entitled MARTIN OF HISTORY, and says) Professor Wesser, what have you to say of this?

Professor: I shall make my comments brief. Without doubt, Martin was a true historical figure of the fourth century AD. He was born of a military family in what is today Yugoslavia, as a boy moved to Northern Italy, and later joined the Roman army stationed in Western France. He became a Christian soon after, later becoming bishop of the territory of Tours, and was responsible for introducing the first monastery to France. He died at the age of 80 and was buried three days later on November 11, 397 AD. (He clears his throat, and continues, speaking rapidly) His value to history you ask? Not much. A big fish in a small pond. The time he lived is a minor period to the scholar, what with the Barbarian invasions and the breakup of Rome taking place at the same time. At best I'd give him a footnote, and as for the picture, it really has no value to me.

Announcer: Thank you, Professor Wesser. (The announcer now tears the picture in two, dropping the pieces on the floor. He picks up the second picture and holds it to view. It reads MARTIN OF LEGEND) Ms. Flash, what have you to say of this?

Ms. Flash: Very inspiring, of course, and all that, but there is really not much I could do with this Martin. Right now Saint Francis has the market tied up for garden statues and bird baths, and with Santa Claus — 'er Saint Nicholas — and St. Patrick, the market won't bear much more. Professor Wesser, is that all we know about this man? Certainly doesn't provide much in the way of local color.

Professor: Well there is the popular legend about the cape...

Ms. Flash: Let's hear it, this may be just what we need!

Professor: Briefly put: one freezing night when Martin was still an unbaptized soldier, he met a beggar freezing in the cold. Martin cut his military cloak in two and gave the beggar half. The following night, Christ appeared to him in a dream and said: "Martin, not-yet-a Christian, it was not a beggar but myself whom you clothed with your cloak."

Ms. Flash: Charming. But unless cloaks come back into fashion there is not much I can do with that. Now let me be frank. We need saints in advertising just like we need mom and apple pie; they add nostalgia and put a little life in the culture. But there's just not much I can do with Martin — he's not worth a cent to me in the present market.

Announcer: Thank you, Ms. Flash. (The announcer tears the picture in two, dropping the pieces on the floor. He then picks up the third picture and holds it out for view. It reads MARTIN OF SCIENCE) Mr. Murk, what have you to say about this?

Mr. Murk: As a social scientist, I am surprised that you ask the question at all. We deal with facts, trends, norms, and concrete numbers — not poetry. Professor Wesser, just what figures *do* we have about this Martin?

Professor: Not much. He lived an estimated 80 years, which by coincidence is the average number of monks housed in his monastery. It is said that there were 2000 people present at his funeral.

Mr. Murk: A little research of my own has turned up not much more. In 1946, six out of every 100 boys in this country were named Martin. The number has since dropped to 5.4. Of 1000 Martin's interviewed, only 12% felt he was a saint, and only half of these had ever heard the story of the cape. In short, Martin is a statistical bust, a tiny pebble on a big beach. Scientifically, he is nothing but a name, and not a very well known one at that! He is worthless to my profession.

Announcer: Thank you Dr. Murk. (He tears picture in half, dropping the pieces to the floor) Ladies and gentlemen, thank you very much for your time and valuable comments. With this we conclude... (this line is said to his microphone. He is interrupted by Mrs. Bee who has walked out to the center, and kneeling down has begun to look through the remains of the pictures. She pulls out a picture that has not been torn and holds it up to view)

Mrs. Bee: Doesn't this belong to anyone? (The picture reads: MARTIN THE HUMAN BEING)

Announcer: I doubt it, Mrs. Bee. What does the picture say?

Mrs. Bee: It says, "Martin, the Human Being." I do apologize for what I'm doing, but I didn't really understand all your fine words. Doesn't anyone want this picture? Or is Martin someone dead and gone?

Professor: We don't even have his tomb, Lady. It was destroyed during the French Revolution!

Mrs. Bee: But is he no more than bones and ashes?

Ms. Flash: Sorry about that, but Martin just won't *sell*!

Mrs. Bee: But he is not an advertising gimmick.

Dr. Murk: Individuals have no statistical worth. Martin does not fit within the parameters of science.

Announcer: Mrs. Bee, just what do you see in this man, Martin, dead now for 1600 years?

Mrs. Bee: I see in Martin just what his picture says: a human being. And I want to remember him just as the Church does because Martin is an instance of what we are and will be: an individual human being who by God's love has been raised up — not lost and forgotten in the shiftings of time — but made living, whole and holy in God.

Readers: O God, by his life and death, Martin offered you worship and praise.

Mrs. Bee: The Martin whom the Church honors is my Martin, a human being, not a pebble on a beach with no meaning, or a mere pretty story. A human being, who lived a long life, in a difficult time, enduring the day to day burdens that we all share, and believing that life has meaning and hope because of Christ, and that at death it is not ended but changed and perfected.

Readers: Holy Lord, God of Might and Power. Blessed is this man Martin who came in the name of the Lord, Hosanna in the highest!

Mrs. Bee: He is not a footnote or a number, but a human being. The Church, because it believes that no one is lost in God's sight, and that God's love is not just a future promise, but something real both in life and after it, proclaims Martin as blessed for all time.

Announcer: Mrs. Bee, I don't think any of us deserve to have that Martin for ourselves. He belongs to you and to all those who have the faith that Martin held.

Professor: Take the picture, Mrs. Bee, it belongs to you.

Ms. Flash: You and the Church deserve it, Mrs. Bee.

Mr. Murk: Someone should celebrate that Saint Martin. Take the picture please.

Mrs. Bee: Thank you very much everyone. We *will* celebrate Saint Martin, we *will*. *(She limps off)*

Narrator: In the Church's Mass on the day recalling St. Martin of Tours, we pray: "O God, by his life and death Martin offered you worship and praise. Help us to do the same." What is true of St. Martin applies equally to all the saints. They show the holy mystery of God's love among us. They remind us of what we are called to be in Christ. (Pause) *The end.*

TURKEY FEATHERS

A Playlet for Thanksgiving
(Middle Grades)

Characters: Narrator
Teacher
Student 1
Student 2
Student 3
Student 4
Student 5
Student 6
Student 7
Student 8
Student 9

Setting: Action begins with STUDENTS 1-6 seated on top altar step. TEACHER stands slightly to their left, with STUDENTS 7-9 offstage right. Narration is read from pulpit.

Narrator: The little story which follows never happened. But it has a good moral for Thanksgiving and we would like to share it with you. The name of our playlet is "Turkey Feathers." (Pause) One day before Thanksgiving the teacher said to her class:

Teacher: Children, I have to leave the room for just a second, and while I'm gone there is a special proj-

ect I want you to work on. I want you to divide into two groups. (six students divide into two groups
of three) Each group will get a large piece of paper,
and on it I want you to draw a picture of a turkey
which represents the meaning of Thanksgiving the
best you can.

Narrator: Then the teacher left the classroom.

Student 1: Quick get the largest piece! (Student 2 grabs
the larger of the two sheets of paper out of the
hand of student 4)

Student 4: I had it first!

Student 2: Too bad, I have it now!

Student 5: Let her have the big piece, it's not worth fighting
about.

Narrator: So the two groups got down to work. No sooner
had they begun, however, than three more students
came into the room; their mother's car had broken
down on the way to school and they were just now
arriving.

Student 9: What are you doing?

Student 3: We're making some turkeys.

Student 9: Can we do it too?

Student 2: You're not getting any paper from us; we want to
win this contest. Go ask the other group.

Narrator: So they went and asked the other children.

Student 9: Can we have some paper to make a turkey?

Student 6: This is the only piece we have. I guess we could cut
off a piece to share with you.

Narrator: So the group which had the smaller piece of paper
made it even smaller and shared with the third
group, which had none at all. Then the teacher returned.

Teacher:	Class, I would now like to see your work to determine who is the winner. Could we see the turkey from group two? (Group 2 hold up their picture)
Teacher:	That's very interesting: would you tell us how your picture expresses the meaning of Thanksgiving?
Student 4:	It's just an ordinary Turkey. I guess it should remind us of the pilgrims or something.
Student 5:	We tried to put a smile on its face to show that Thanksgiving is a holiday.
Student 6:	But otherwise, we just didn't have much chance to think of any special meaning.
Teacher:	Very good; now could we hear from group one? (Group 1 holds up turkey picture. It shows a very large turkey, filling the entire piece of paper)
Teacher:	Would someone explain how *your* picture expresses the meaning of Thanksgiving?
Student 1:	We drew the biggest, fattest turkey we could, to remind us that Thanksgiving is a day of plenty.
Student 2:	Yes, plenty of *food*: cranberry sauce, pumpkin pie, and especially *turkey!*
Student 3:	We even gave our turkey a name, *Gobble* turkey, because on Thanksgiving we can eat as much as we want!
Teacher:	Well, of the two groups, I'll have to admit that you did the best ... (group three emerges from the side with something in their hands) Oh, did you students make something too?
Student 1:	(To Student 2) There is no way they can win. They only have little pieces of paper!
Teacher:	Could you explain what you have done?
Student 7:	We didn't have much to work with, so we decided not to make a turkey of our own.

Student 8:	Instead, we thought we would do something to show how grateful we were to the group who shared some of their paper with us.
Student 9:	We made feathers for their turkey. Each feather stands for something for which we are thankful to God. (Each student attaches a feather to the turkey as he or she explains its meaning)
Student 7:	The green feather is a reminder of all things living, forests, green lawns, and plants. It tells us that all growth is a gift of God.
Student 8:	The red feather reminds us of things that are warm and cheery, of sunsets on summer days, and warm fires in the fireplaces when it's rainy. Most of all it reminds us of warm and caring people, and God's love for all of us.
Student 9:	The blue feather reminds us of the mystery of life, of the sky that stretches on forever, and of the huge oceans. It reminds us of everything about life which we don't understand, and of the mystery of God himself who became man in Jesus.
Student 7:	As for the other colors, we didn't give a meaning to them. Because each of us has so many special things that he or she can thank God for, and we wanted to remind us of that. (Students 7, 8, & 9 now add on another set of feathers in different colors)
Narrator:	And then the teacher told the class:
Teacher:	Not everyone will celebrate the same Thanksgiving tomorrow. For some people Thanksgiving will be like the fat turkey, for others it will be like the turkey with the feathers. Each of you has to make up his or her mind which it shall be.
Narrator:	The teacher never did tell the children who won the contest. She hung up both of the pictures for the rest of the day for the students to look at and

decide which Thanksgiving they wished to cele-brate. (Pause) *The end.*

Additional Notes:

The turkey pictures should be prepared ahead of time. During the first part of the playlet, actors should take care that the congregation only see the clean side of the paper or cardboard.

The colored feathers should also be prepared in advance, with tape attached to them for fastening to the turkey of group 2.

THE STORY CONTEST

A Playlet for the Last Sunday
of the Church Year
(Middle Grades)

Characters: Announcer
First Child
Second Child
Third Child
Three or four other children (Group)

Setting: Students sit in a row across top altar step. They begin in a reflective mood, eyes cast downward.

Announcer: The name of our playlet is "The Story Contest." (Pause) Once some children got together and told three stories about the world and how it will end. The first story they did not really understand. The second made them afraid. The third story made them feel loved — and that is the reason for our play.

Group: (They look up at the congregation, and say, quietly but clearly)
Tell us a story,
What do you say?
What can you share
With us today?

First Child: (Very slowly) This is my story. I heard it from a man on television. It is about the world and how it will end. (Pause) The world is really just a big gob that fell together one day and floated out between the stars. From this gob things sprung out that wriggled. Things like bugs and frogs and people. Someday the world with everything on it will fall into a black hole and be gone, or break up into a million bits and never be seen again.

Announcer: But the children didn't understand the story. They felt that their world was too beautiful to be only a gob. They thought people were more than frogs and bugs. So the second child was invited to tell his/her story.

Group: (Quietly but clearly)
Tell us a story,
What do you say?
What can you share
With us today?

Second Child: (Very slowly) This is my story. I saw it in a movie. It is about the world and how it will end. There was once this world alone in space. It went on its way for millions of years, spinning and spinning. The inhabitants of the world all this time kept waiting to hear someone tell them why they were there. Then one day an *Alien Force* arrived. It was more powerful than anyone could imagine. It tore down all the stars from the sky and snuffed out the sun. The *Alien Force* turned most people into slaves, and anyone left turned into a mutant.

Announcer: But the children didn't like the story. It made them afraid. They already felt weak and small, and they were afraid that something like that might really happen — and they wouldn't be able to do anything about it. (Pause) So they invited the third child to tell his/her story.

Group: (Quietly but clearly)
Tell us a story
What do you say?
What can you share
With us today?

Third Child: (Very slowly) This is my story. It's not just a story, because it's true. There was once this world that floated in the sky and spun for millions of years. And God held it in the palm of His hand, and entered into it and loved it. And some people knew that God had loved it with a love stronger than death. And some people knew this and called Him Jesus, and some didn't. And finally one day, God said *STOP*. The world seemed to stop spinning, and because God was speaking no one noticed the sun or the stars. Then God said: "Children, since your world began, I have held you in the palm of my hand, and I have loved you through my only Son with a love stronger than death. Now at last I want *everyone* to see this love and be with me in a world that never ends.

Announcer: The children liked the third story, because they no longer felt confused or afraid, but loved. They knew it was their story, because the person the story came from was not someone in a movie or on television, but Jesus himself. They knew it was their story, because it was true. *The end.*

GABRIEL AND MARY

A Feast of Mary
(Grades 5-7)

Characters:	Narrator
	Gabriel
	Mary
	Mr. X (No lines)
	Mrs. A
	Mr. B
	Mrs. C

Narrator: Our Gospel playlet is called "Gabriel and Mary." It's a what-if story. What if the angel Gabriel and Mary came back to pay the world a visit after all these years? That's where we begin.

Mary: Well if it isn't the angel Gabriel. You look exhausted!

Gabriel: Mary, you are my favorite human being, but I have had it with you earthlings. I have been wandering around here all day trying to drum up some enthusiasm for Advent, and all I am getting for my efforts is a headache.

Mary: I don't understand, Gabriel.

Gabriel: Let me try just one more time, then you'll see. Maybe I have forgotten how to do it, but when I

	came to tell you some Good News many years ago, I didn't have any trouble. Here comes somebody. This was my original approach.
Mr. X:	(Comes walking by)
Gabriel:	Excuse me, I would like to ask you something about ...
Mr. X:	(Walks on past Gabriel without stopping)
Gabriel:	So I changed my approach.
Mrs. A:	(Comes walking rapidly across the stage. Gabriel claps hands and then points them toward Mrs. A, freezing her in her tracks).
Gabriel:	Even then, you can't stop people these days. Listen: (he turns up an imaginary volume knob).
Mrs. A:	If I can get that loan at 15 percent interest, then make the sales meeting in the city, I'll be just in time for the 3 PM flight to the convention in Salt Lake City ...
Gabriel:	(Again claps hands and points them toward Mrs. A, as her voice trails off into silence) Oops, here come two more!
Mr. B:	(Crosses stage, is stopped by Gabriel; volume is turned up) I can hardly wait to get my hands on that ZX-7 turbo car. It has a digital dashboard and bucket seats. My friends won't know what to say ...
Gabriel:	(Turns off Mr. B — Mrs. C walks across stage and is stopped by Gabriel's hand clap)
Mrs. C:	One bill after another, I just don't know how I'll pay the rent and support my family, and now the company is starting to lay off workers because of poor sales ... (Gabriel stops her)
Mary:	Well, Gabriel, you've got their attention, now what?
Gabriel:	Once I've got them to stop thinking, I still can't get anywhere. Watch: Folks, let me ask you a ques-

tion. Advent is the time in which we prayerfully await the coming of the Lord. What does this season mean to you?

Mrs. A: I don't have time for that — I have my own thoughts to concern myself about.

Mr. B: It really doesn't touch me one way or another — who cares?

Mrs. C: I can't handle the idea of waiting for the Lord. I don't have any space for that.

Gabriel: I give up! (He flops down onto the top altar step)

Mary: Gabriel, maybe the problem is that you don't understand people well enough. Let's look down into the deepest levels of their hearts and see what they are really saying (Mary turns the imaginary knob)

Mrs. A: I feel empty and terribly afraid, as if life were a huge question for which there is no answer.

Mr. B: I feel lost and as if no one could ever love me for what I am. I don't know where to turn and I am afraid to ask.

Mrs. C: I feel a sense of deep loneliness that all the success in the world can never make up for.

Gabriel: (to Mary) What happens now?

Mary: You can speak the Good News to them — they have to listen to hear it.

Gabriel: Friends, once I told Mary here that she was graced among all other human beings and that the Lord was with her. Now, because her Son came to us once and for all, you are all blessed, and safe in God's love. Thinking about Christ coming into our lives is what Advent is all about.

Mary: Very Good, Gabriel. But now that you have implanted the idea, you must let them go: they have to make it their own way by themselves.

Gabriel: Let's hope this works. (He begins turning up the imaginary knob. At a certain point, Mrs. A, Mr. B, and Mrs. C all begin talking as before. They speak simultaneously)

Mr. B: I can hardly wait to get my hands on that ZX-7 turbo car. It has a digital dashboard and bucket seats. My friends won't know what to say ...

Mrs. A: If I can get that loan at 15 percent interest, then make the sales meeting in the city, I'll be just in time for the 3 PM flight to the convention in Salt Lake City ...

Mrs. C: One bill after another, I just don't know how I'll pay the rent and support my family, and now the company is starting to lay off workers because of poor sales ...

Gabriel: (Growing angry) I've had it with you people! Go away! (He claps his hand, shakes them at the characters, who immediately begin walking off in three directions, while continuing to repeat their lines) Why does anyone even bother...

Mary: Gabriel, look! One of them has stopped.

Mrs. C: (has begun walking back to Gabriel, then stops, turns and walks over to microphone at the center of the top altar step. She acts confused, lost. Finally, she speaks) O Lord, you know it has been a busy time for me, and I've forgotten all about you. Help me to have a place in my heart for you during this time of Advent. (She pauses briefly, then resumes and walks briskly off) One bill after another, I don't know how I'll pay...

Gabriel: She did change! If I hadn't seen it with my own eyes I never would have believed it. But what about the others?

Mary: God knocks gently on the door of every human being's heart, Gabriel. Whether they choose to open that door is up to them. But I think you have done your good deed for the day. Maybe we should go back to heaven for a while and give things time to work.

Narrator: And so Gabriel ended his day on earth, having learned both about the mystery of the human heart and the greater mystery of God's love. *The end.*

BIRTHDAYS ARE BETTER

A Dramatic Sketch for Advent
(Middle Grades)

Characters: Judy Rebmann, a ten year old girl
Richard Stuart, a ten year old boy

Setting: The story takes place on a hilltop overlooking a city. When the playlet begins, JUDY is seated, enthralled by the sight spread out before her. RICHARD enters from left. He appears to be munching a cookie.

Judy: Hi. (Nervously) Merry Christmas.

Richard: Hi.

Judy: (After an embarrassing pause) What...what's *your* name?

Richard: No, you tell me.

Judy: (Matter of factly) I asked first.

Richard: (He sits down beside Judy, still eating his cookie): My name is Richard Stuart Junior. That's because my father's name is Richard Stuart. What's your name?

Judy: Judy Rebmann.

Richard: How old are you? I'm ten. (Takes out another cookie and begins eating.)

Judy:	(Showing no interest) I'm ten, too. (She pauses) Isn't it pretty up here? Look at all the houses down there. There must be thousands of them, all with tiny roofs and lawns (her voice fades off).
Richard:	(Not at all poetic) I've flown in an airplane before. Then everything is *really* small. But you get used to it.
Judy:	I wouldn't. Everyday I come up here to the top of the hill and I never get used to it.
Richard:	You're lucky — I wish I could.
Judy:	Could I have a cookie? (Richard hesitates then takes one from his pocket and gives it to her. She takes a bite and resumes the conversation) Won't your parents let you come up here?
Richard:	Oh, I do what I want. But three years ago we moved out to the valley. We used to live right down there, but the neighborhood started to go bad, so we moved out. My Uncle Jack said it didn't make any difference *who* lived next to him.
Judy:	Your Uncle Jack still lives down there?
Richard:	Uncle Jack is my father's brother. We only come to see him once a year on his birthday. What an awful time to have your birthday: the day before Christmas!
Judy:	Yeah...
Richard:	Uncle Jack *makes* us come over. That's what he calls his "Christmas present from us." At least we only have to see him once a year.
Judy:	Can I have another cookie?
Richard:	(Takes another cookie from his pocket and gives it to her) They're from his party. All the old people got beer and cheese and I got cookies. Then they started arguing again. Everyone telling Uncle Jack that he's crazy not to move out of the neighborhood.

Judy:	But why did you come up here?
Richard:	So I won't have to listen to my folks and relatives.
Judy:	(There is an awkward silence for a moment, then) Sometimes I want to get away from things too. But most of the time, its nature that brings me. When the wind is blowing, and the clouds slide across the sky, its almost as if... as if the world itself were breathing out a special poem or prayer.
Richard:	Yeah. (He hesitates then goes on) I hate it when grown-ups start fighting. When we drove up the driveway, it was all smiles, "Merry Christmas and Happy Birthday, Uncle Jack." They're only pretending. Mom and Dad wanted me to sing "Happy Birthday" to him, but *they* wouldn't do it!
Judy:	When do you have to be back?
Richard:	They'll be at it until dark, I guess. Maybe the television will have a football game on and they won't have to talk to each other.
Judy:	Do you have hills where you live now?
Richard:	Not in the middle of the valley: (he points) over there somewhere.
Judy:	Across the river?
Richard:	*Way* over. You must have been there.
Judy:	No.
Richard:	Don't you drive around? We do. Whenever we get a new car. Me, my mom and dad. It's a lot of fun, the first time.
Judy:	My grandmother and I were going to walk down to Five-points to look at the decorations, but she hurt her leg.
Richard:	Well, why don't you take the bus?
Judy:	We just don't.

Richard: You're stupid. All you need is money. (He takes an exasperated breath) My father is vice-president of the Mount Sheridan Company, and I get everything I want. You should see the dirt bike I got this year for Christmas.

Judy: But Christmas isn't 'til tomorrow.

Richard: At our house, Santa Claus comes when the United Parcel Serviceman arrives. It's too much trouble for Mom to try to hide all my stuff. I had a great Christmas this year, and Dad promised me a pony next year if his real estate pays off. What did you get?

Judy: I don't know.

Richard: You sure do things funny at your house.

Judy: Grandma says there's a reason to keep secrets when Christmas comes. It's the celebration of the best suprise present God ever gave the world.

Richard: Well, my Mom gave Dad a Cadillac Coupe De Ville this year.

Judy: Wow, that's really doing Christmas up in a big way.

Richard: Sorta'. But Mom always gives Dad a Coupe De Ville for Christmas. After a while they all seem the same except for the upholstery.

Judy: My grandmother gave me a kitten once for Christmas...but the kitten ran away. Do you have any pets?

Richard: (Nodding yes) Mmm (He stands up holding his stomach) I'm sick of cookies...have another one. (He gives her a cookie).

Judy: Thanks.

Richard: (He stamps his feet) It's getting cold up here. I think I'd better be going back.

Judy:	I guess you'll have a real happy Christmas.
Richard:	I sure will, if I get that pony.
Judy:	(Pauses briefly, lost in thought) You know — sometimes I think Christmas is the best time of the *whole* year.
Richard:	(Starts to walk off, then turns and says) Yeah — but sometimes *birthdays* are better.
Note:	As originally presented, actors sat on back of organ, at side of sanctuary, lit by a single spot light shining up from below them.
	The sketch can be done as a dramatic reading.

WATCHERS IN THE HILLS
A Dramatic Sketch for Advent
(Junior High Level)

Characters: Commentator
Rebecca
Deborah
Judah
Benjamin

Setting: A single flood lamp, covered with a red gel, on the floor of the sanctuary facing upward. SHEPHERDS sit on the top altar steps.

Commentator: Our dramatic sketch takes place on a hilltop overlooking Bethlehem during the time of Caesar Augustus. We find three shepherds seated around a campfire warming themselves against the chill of the winter night. Suddenly they hear something move in the darkness.

Benjamin: Judah? Is that you? (Benjamin is afraid of robbers or worse)

Rebecca: (Peering off into the darkness) It looks like Judah. I think I recognize his walk.

Deborah: (Also afraid) Make certain, Benjamin! These hills are a danger at this time of night!

Benjamin: (Loudly) Judah, Son of Joshua, is that you coming up the slope?

Judah: (Entering from right. He seems to be in a daze) It is I, Judah. (He limps in, seats himself at the fire, and warms his hands as the rest look on. Finally he continues to speak) I bring no good news. Those two sheep that were missing from the flock this afternoon — I found them. Their remains, that is. Half-way between here and the high road to Bethlehem, in the ashes of a fireside already cold. Those no good travellers filling the roads this winter are to blame.

Rebecca: We are cursed, we are! Accursed! Three lambs eaten by wild dogs last week. Now this. Mark my words: we will be chewing leaves and roots soon, if more of the flock is lost.

Benjamin: Yes, we *are* cursed. But the world is cursed with us as well. The travellers on the high-road were probably as hungry as we soon shall be.

Rebecca: Didn't give 'em any right to make off with our sheep! See this staff? (She holds up a rough branch) If I caught them I would have used it, I tell you!

Benjamin: Any of the hill shepherds would. Look across the night. It must be twenty or thirty fires such as ours that I can see. Each surrounded by wretched shepherds like ourselves. Any one of them would have used his club.

Rebecca: Mankind is cursed. We scrape and claw to survive, and we do it over one another.

Deborah: (There is a pause, finally Deborah speaks) But it is not all bad. There are the grand market days and the festivals.

Rebecca: Pshaw! What does it get us, child? A half a day of feast and two months sitting out here shivering in the cold. Life is damned from the beginning and the only miracle that has ever occurred is the fact that people put up with living at all!

Benjamin: Rebecca has reason. You live in Bethlehem, the city, you've got taxes and noise. You slave in the fields, you've got hunger and robbers. It's always like that. It always will be. Things have no meaning.

Deborah: But they must! Forget your cold and your empty stomach for an instant. Look above us at the canopy of the heavens, see the fires shining in the night across the hills, and the walls of Bethlehem silvery in the moonlight. Surely the world is a stage for some great performance, even if we do not know what it is.

Rebecca: Listen to the girl! Five sheep lost in less than ten days and she speaks of moonlight and stars. Man's lot on earth is to suffer the change of seasons, watch the sun rise and set, pass his time in ill-health and suffering, only to die away to that same nothingness from which he came. Who but an insane dreamer could pretend there might be more, that this could somehow change?

Benjamin: (There is a moment of silence while her words slowly sink in. Then Benjamin turns to Judah, who has been lost in thought throughout the conversation) Judah, what is it? You have said not a word since you returned from finding the dead sheep.

Deborah: Silence is wisdom when there is foolish talk about.

Judah: (Apologizing) I am sorry. I was not paying attention. My mind has been taken with something I saw and *seem* to have heard just as I reached the crest at the head of the valley on my way back here. There were dozens of shepherd fires across the hills just as you see here. But then suddenly over one of them in the far distance, I thought I saw the sky light up almost as day — and it seemed, though perhaps I was only dreaming, that I heard music —

heavenly music — and then suddenly it all stopped, and for the life that is in me, I do not know what it was or why...

Rebecca: (There is a long pause before she finally comments) Whatever it was, it is gone. And things will go on their muddled way as always.

Benjamin: Rebecca, you are too hard in your heart. (He speaks wistfully) When I was young, I used to wonder at the glory of the stars. Like Deborah, I, too, felt that somewhere in the universe there must be meaning, that somehow all things would be brought together and life renewed. (He pauses and then concludes abruptly) But not in these forsaken hills will anything ever happen that could do this. Not in a million years. *That* I can assure you.

Deborah: (Again after a pause) Oh, but something *could* happen. I do not know what or why. But the world is too grand and mysterious a place to be left forever alone, without meaning or purpose.

Benjamin: Then dream on with Judah, Deborah. As for me, the world is what it is. And not all the lights of heaven, nor an act of God himself could ever change it...*The end.*

THE FORGIVING FATHER

A Playlet for Penitential Times
(Primary Grades)

Characters:	First Reader
	Second Reader
	Little Son
	Big Son
	Father
Setting:	Actors stand/sit on top altar steps to the side of altar when not reciting their lines. Ideally two microphones are used. A serape type stole made from pieces of brightly colored cloth is set off to one side.
1st Reader:	This is a story Jesus told his friends one day. It is called "The Forgiving Father." (Pause) Once there was a kind old man who had two sons. One was big and one was little. Everything seemed fine until the little son said to his Father:
Little Son:	Dad, it is getting very boring around here. I want all my money so I can take a *long* vacation.
1st Reader:	So the Father took all the money the family had in the bank and gave a big chunk of it to the Little Son.

2nd Reader: The Little Son went far away to a big city. He rented an apartment, bought a shiny red car, and had parties day and night. Then he ran out of money.

1st Reader: All his friends left him, and wouldn't even give him food. Luckily for the Little Son, he found a job feeding pigs.

2nd Reader: Even then he was hungry, and winter was coming on. At last he came to his senses:

Little Son: This is awful. I don't have my red car, my friends have left me. The pigs get better food than I do. I will have to go back to my Father and say, "Dad, I did a very, very bad thing. Please forgive me and let me live at home again, even as a hired hand!"

1st Reader: And so he trudged home. But when the Little Son was still far away, his Father saw him coming and ran down the road to meet him.

Little Son: Dad, I did a very, very bad thing. Please forgive me and let me live at home again, even as a hired hand!

2nd Reader: But the Father said to his servants:

Father: Quick, bring out my best coat and put it on him. Buy him some new pants and a new pair of shoes. Tell the cook to prepare a *banquet*. We will celebrate because my Little Son was dead and has come back to life! He was lost and I have found him again!

(The Father places the colored stole over the neck and shoulders of his son)

1st Reader: Then the celebration began. But the Big Son was very angry when he got home and found out what was happening.

Big Son: I am going to stay out here on the front steps and not go in. I am *so* angry I cannot believe it!

Father: Son, please come in for the party. Your brother is home at last!

Big Son: Dad, I worked for you all this time. I always did everything you told me to do. But I never got a party like this. Now after my little brother has gone and wasted everything you gave him, you do this for him!

Father: Don't be sad, Big Son. Smile and be happy. Everything I own is yours and you know that. But we must celebrate. Your little brother seemed dead, but now he has come back to life. He was lost and we have found him again!
(Pause)

The end.

DO THIS IN MEMORY OF ME: THE MASS THROUGH THE AGES

**Votive Mass of the Holy Eucharist
(Junior High Level)**

Parts: Up to thirteen narrators may be used for the text, which is intended to accompany a presentation of student art work projected either as slides or as transparencies with an opaque projector.

The history of the Mass: A SLIDE PRESENTATION

SLIDE 1: The Mass is the central sacrament of our Catholic faith. It is a symbol of the Church's unity, the source of her strength and life.

SLIDE 2: At the Last Supper, Jesus broke bread, blessed it, and gave it to his disciples, with the instructions, "Do this in memory of me." Across nineteen centuries, his followers have faithfully celebrated this event, just as we do tonight/this morning.

SLIDE 3: What is the Mass? No single definition is complete. But one way of describing it is as "a remembering service." The Christian community gathers to recall Christ's saving deeds: his life, death on the cross, and resurrection. Because the Mass is a sacrament, that is, an action of Christ who remains with his people, it is much more than a commemoration. When we celebrate the Eucharist, we are actually present at Christ's crucifixion on the hill at Calvary and at his rising from the tomb three days later.

SLIDE 4:   The significance of the Mass is one and unchanging. But its ritual, or outward forms, have not always been as we know them today. During the time of the early Christians, the blessing and breaking of the bread by the priest took place after a dinner banquet at someone's home. There was no permanent altar, and the prayers of the Mass were partly improvised.

SLIDE 5:   Prior to the year 300 AD we know few details about the Mass and how it changed. We do know it was not the same everywhere, and with the passing of time there was a gradual trend to standardize prayers, gestures, and even the calendar of feast days.

SLIDE 6:   When the emperor Constantine made Christianity the official religion of the Roman Empire, important changes soon resulted. For the first time, large buildings were built especially for worship, and a stone altar became a common feature. Mass became solemn, and the community remained standing for the entire service, but now only the clergy were allowed in the area near the altar.

SLIDE 7:   Originally, churches did not possess tabernacles. But in order to have the Holy Eucharist available for the sick and the dying, it became the practice to set aside some consecrated bread in a side chapel after Mass. Then, sometime in the fourth or fifth century, a lamp began to be left burning before the Eucharist as a sign to the people of Christ's continuing presence. The vestments of the priest, which were originally those worn by ordinary people, were left unchanged, and as new fashions appeared, the vestments began to appear more and more distinctive.

SLIDE 8:   Communities began to copy more and more the prayers and the gestures of the Bishop of Rome. Not all did this, however. This explains why today there are several different styles of celebrating Mass, such as the rites of the Eastern Orthodox, the Coptic Church of Africa, and the form used by the City of Milan in Italy. Even though most Catholics today continue to follow the Roman Rite, the others are all valid forms of celebrating the Eucharist.

SLIDE 9:   During the Middle Ages emphasis was placed on the Mass as the making-present of Christ's sacrifice on the cross rather than as a celebration of Christ's ongoing presence in the community. The altar at times became lost behind elaborate decorations. Singing was not by the congregation but by special choirs. This form of celebration did not seem strange to people living in a world of distant kings and wealthy nobles. They thought of Christ as their king and Lord. This shows us how in different times, the Mass has changed to fit the mentality of the age.

SLIDE 10:   In the 1500s as a result of the Protestant Reformation, many communities did away with the Mass entirely, removing all decoration from churches and discarding vestments. They focused their attention instead on remembering Christ through Bible readings, prayer, and sermons.

SLIDE 11:   The holy father at that time, Pope Paul III, called together the Council of Trent to respond to this situation. Among the many things the Council did was to set down a form for celebrating the Eucharist, which remained almost unchanged for the next 400 years. The Latin Mass of the Council of Trent lasted until the Second Vatican Council called by Pope John XXIII in our own times.

SLIDE 12:   The Second Vatican Council did many things both to restore the original simplicity of the Mass and to make it more modern. One of these reforms was to allow national languages to be used in place of Latin, the language of the liturgy which had been in use since the first centuries of the Church. For some of those who grew up to the beautiful, rhythmical sounds of old Latin prayers, their passing was a sad thing.

SLIDE 13:   But the world had changed, and while the rite of the Mass continued to be as always the remembering celebration of Christ's life, death, and resurrection, the Mass had also changed to suit the needs of the Christian community better. *The end.*

Slide descriptions: (These are suggestions only. Students might be invited to come up with other ideas based on the reading)

Slide 1: Chalice and large host
Slide 2: The Last Supper
Slide 3: Christ teaching, a triptych showing Christ as a teacher, Christ on the cross, and Christ rising from the dead
Slide 4: Early Christians gathered around a table
Slide 5: A priest in chasuble with arms outstretched
Slide 6: A large Church with community standing before altar
Slide 7: A tabernacle light (burning candle)
Slide 8: Priests in different styles/colors of vestments
Slide 9: The altar partially obscured by flowers and an altar screen
Slide 10: The Book of Scripture
Slide 11: Priest celebrating Mass with his back to the congregation
Slide 12: Priest celebrating Mass today
Slide 13: The Eucharist and chalice radiating light

GIOVANNI AND THE POPES

A playlet for the Feast of a Pope
(Junior High)

Characters: Announcer
Giovanni
Pope Pius XI
Pope Urban V
Pope Sergius III
St. Peter

Setting: When the Gospel has been read, all house lights go *off*. A microphone and a floor lamp are set up before the celebrant's chair and the front center altar platform. All is in darkness as the ANNOUNCER steps up to the podium, turns on the podium light, and begins to read.

Announcer: The mother Church of all the Catholic churches in the world is the Church of St. John Lateran. Imagine that we are in this enormous Roman Church, that it is evening, and that only the vigil light is burning. This is the setting for our presentation: *Giovanni and the Popes.*
(Ghostly music comes on softly)
Our story takes place on the night of November 11, the vigil of the Feast of the Basilica. A poor Roman beggar named Giovanni has had just a lit-

tle too much to drink and now finds himself locked within the great empty church.
(Ghostly music swells louder. Altar platform light goes on)

Giovanni: (Enters from side, makes his way hesitantly to top altar step where he flops down on the ground) O Mary and all the saints, what have I done tonight? (hic) Came in here for a little nap — now the place is locked up tight as a drum; everybody gone home. (Pauses then shouts out) Hello, anyone in here? (hic) Beh, what have I done? Giovanni's not a bad Catholic. Not a good one either (hic) but I must deserve better than being tombed up for the night with all these icy statues and cold stones. Don't know what time it is, or how long I've been asleep. (Calling out) Hello! Won't someone let me out of this place! Coming in, saw the poster on the wall — tomorrow — Feast of St. John Lateran. "Our celebration" it said. Beh, the only thing I'll celebrate is not catching pneumonia!
(Ghostly music. Pope Pius XI wearing a tall bishop's miter appears at the celebrant's chair. Floor light here goes on)

Giovanni: Wait a minute (hic), am I dreaming or drunker than I think? Who are you? What's your name?

Pius XI: My name is "Pius," the eleventh to bear that name. The two-hundred and fifty-eighth Pope in the line of Peter.

Giovanni: You seem to be a little early for what they are calling "our celebration." Is that why you're here at this hour?

Pius XI: This is where my chair was placed, the symbol of my priestly presence. It was here that I signed a treaty with the government of Italy in 1929, restoring these sacred walls to the ownership of the Universal Church.

Giovanni:	That's very nice, your excellency (hic), but it doesn't really move me too much. You want to celebrate and I want to get out of here.
Pius:	But it is "our celebration," Giovanni. It was here that I presided over all the Churches of the world, and with God's help kept firm the faith in the risen Lord. (Light goes out)
Giovanni:	But nothing to do with Giovanni. (Pause) Beh. Now where has he gone? Why didn't I ask him for a key? (Yawn) Perhaps I can sleep the night through (Yawn), I am so *very* tired. (Ghostly music. Pope Pius XI has left the celebrant's chair. Now seated there is Pope Urban V, also wearing a tall bishop's miter. Floor light goes on)
Giovanni:	Oops! I thought I heard footsteps. (He calls off in the direction opposite the celebrant's chair) Hello! Anyone here?
Urban V:	Yes, my son?
Giovanni:	(Looks back the opposite direction in surprise) Oh! (hic) Who are you?
Urban V:	My name is Urban, the fifth to bear that name. I was the Pope, the one hundred and ninety-ninth bishop of Rome in the line of Peter the Apostle. I have come to celebrate our feast tomorrow with you.
Giovanni:	You don't seem too happy, Pope. I mean, this party tomorrow may not interest me, but you must have memories of this place?
Urban:	Giovanni, this Church is the symbol of my duty as Pope, for it is here where my chair is found, the symbol of my office as bishop of Rome. When this great Church building burnt down in 1360, I rebuilt it.
Giovanni:	Then why so glum?

Urban: Because it is also a sign of weakness. I lived here only a few years. I preferred to work from my palace in France, where there were fewer problems.

Giovanni: But did you do your job?

Urban: I guess I did, in the important things. I presided over the unity of all the churches, I preached the Gospel, and kept firm the people in the faith of the risen Lord...

Giovanni: Why (hic) of course you did, Urban. I'm sure all the popes who came after your time will be happy to see you ... I mean (hic) I'm (hic) even happy to see you. (Pause) You wouldn't be able to get me out of here (Urban's spotlight goes off) would you? (Pause) Pope Urban? (Pause) Anyone here? (Silence) Oh well (yawn) ... off to sleep.
(Giovanni sleeps. Ghostly music)
(Pope Sergius takes his place at the celebrant's chair. His spotlight goes on)

Sergius: (Gruffly, to Giovanni) On your knees in my presence!

Giovanni: (Dazed, still sitting): Uh (hic) a ... what?

Sergius: On your knees! What is your name? Who are you?

Giovanni: (Standing, tottering) I'm Giovanni, a beggar. (Sniffs disdainfully) You are certainly gruffy tonight. Not like the others.

Sergius: (Proudly, in a militaristic manner) I am Sergius, the third, Bishop of Rome, one-hundred and twentieth in the line of St. Peter. I lived in an age of blood and iron.

Giovanni: (Still stunned by the Pope's forceful way of speaking) Oh ... I see.

Sergius: Rome was a battlefield of feuding families. I regained my rightful place with my own army of roughnecks. (Pauses for a moment, to look about the church as if inspecting it) The old place is looking good, my beggar. It had been knocked down by an earthquake shortly before I arrived. I rebuilt it, I made my palace on these grounds.

Giovanni: (Tottering slightly) Things must have been different then ...

Sergius: (Firmly) Yes, Giovanni!

Giovanni: May I please sit down and go back to sleep?

Sergius: (Jolts his head back sharply as if insulted, looks Giovanni over carefully, then then says) You *may* sit down.
(Spotlight on Sergius goes out. Ghostly music)

Giovanni: (Mumbling to himself) Thank you (yawn, hic). I'm really having a difficult night, your highness, or ... your holiness, or ... whatever ... (he is asleep).
(Ghostly music continues for a brief moment. Peter enters from side of the altar area. He walks up and sits beside Giovanni. Unlike the other Popes, he holds his miter in his hands)

Peter: (Hesitantly) Excuse me, I think I may be lost, I'm not sure. Could you tell me where I am?

Giovanni: (Rubbing his eyes) You're in the very old and very cold church of St. John Lateran. Who are you?

Peter: My name is Peter. I was a fisherman by trade — at first, anyway.

Giovanni: (Horrified that Peter is next to him and not over at the celebrant's chair as were all the other Popes) What are you doing *here* and not over (gesturing) *there*?

Peter: I'm not sure. There is a celebration of some sort I'm supposed to attend ... maybe I misunderstood. I used to lead a little group of Christians in this city a long time ago. In a way I was sort of a cornerstone of things here. That is, 'til I was put to

	death on a cross. I wasn't sure about whether I deserved to die in the same manner as my Lord Jesus ... so they turned me upside down.
Giovanni:	Peter, you don't seem to be sure about a lot of things.
Peter:	Yes, I always was like that. This thing in my hand here (gesturing toward the miter), not too sure about what to do with this either. Maybe I'm in the wrong place ... maybe I should ...
Giovanni:	(Interrupting strongly) Peter! This is crazy! Now just pull yourself together. Look at yourself! What are you doing here in the middle of the Church? Get over to that chair where you belong! (He walks Peter over to the chair. Peter is shy, Giovanni is clearly still drunk by the way he walks)
Peter:	But I never saw this chair before!
Giovanni:	Of course you haven't. It's a symbol. Popes come and go, but whatever you were about remains.
Peter:	And what of this vast building?
Giovanni:	It's a sign that God's love is strong and forever. Now look, Peter, I've been up all night and there's a few things I've learned by this time. (Turning to the miter) Put this thing on your head, like everyone else.
Peter:	Giovanni, I'm just a poor, weak man.
Giovanni:	You have a lot of company, from what I've seen.
Peter:	And there is no reason to celebrate.
Giovanni:	There is plenty! Now stand up straight, hold your head up. Repeat after me: My name is Peter!
Peter:	(Weakly) My name is ...
Giovanni:	Say it loud and strong, so your successors will recognize you. Say it strong like a rock! My name is Peter, First Bishop of Rome.
Peter:	MY NAME IS PETER, FIRST BISHOP OF ROME.
Giovanni:	Chosen by Christ to preside over the unity of all the Churches.

Peter: CHOSEN BY CHRIST TO PRESIDE OVER THE UNITY OF ALL THE CHURCHES.

Giovanni: That a-way, Peter, you're doing great! I preached the Gospel.

Peter: I PREACHED THE GOSPEL.

Giovanni: And I kept the people firm in the faith of Christ, the risen Lord.

Peter: AND I KEPT THE PEOPLE FIRM IN THE FAITH OF CHRIST, THE RISEN LORD.

(As Peter has been proclaiming, Giovanni has been slowly backing away from him to the center of the altar area. Now he dashes back to his side, clapping his hands as he does so)

Giovanni: (He talks quickly, his voice fading off) That's better, that's better!

Peter: Giovanni, will I be the only one here?

Giovanni: Of course not. You won't believe those celebrating this day. I'll be here, and then there's all your successors, hundreds of them, and the universal Church throughout the world. Let me tell you about Sergius ... he was bishop ...

Announcer: (While the voice of Giovanni fades out) And so, the poor Giovanni narrated to Peter all he had learned. The feast day was not only the celebration of the popes who had been connected with the Church through the years, but the feast of everyone, including Giovanni — including you and me. *The end.*

THE GOOD SHEPHERD AND HIS SHEEP

A Playlet for a Sunday of the Year
(Primary Grades)

Characters:	Narrator Shepherd Hired Hand Wolf Sheep (divided into 2 flocks)
Setting:	Action takes place on top altar step using one microphone for the GOOD SHEPHERD and another for the HIRED HAND and WOLF.
Narrator:	God looks after each of us just as carefully as a good shepherd looks after his sheep. This is what the following story, based on today's Gospel, tells us.
	(SHEEP and Shepherd enter)
Shepherd:	I am the Good Shepherd, and these are my sheep.
Sheep:	Jesus is the Good Shepherd, and we are his sheep. He loves us and cares for us.
	(More Sheep and Hired Hand enter)
Hired Hand:	I am a hired hand. I don't own these sheep, but it's an easy job.

Sheep
(of 2nd flock): The hired hand is our shepherd, and he is not much help, especially when a wolf comes.

Hired Hand: Did you say a wolf was coming? Sheep, I'll see you later! (He runs off).

Wolf: I am the wolf. I shall chase these sheep all over the countryside. Watch! (He growls)

(All the sheep of the hired hand scatter in different directions, saying)

Sheep: Help, help; save us! Eeek.

Wolf: (To sheep of the Good Shepherd) Why don't you run away too?

Shepherd: They are not afraid because they know I am the Good Shepherd, who loves and cares for them.

Wolf: The Good Shepherd, eh? Prove it!

Shepherd: I know each of my sheep by name. I call them and they follow me. This one is Sandra, this one is John, this one is Mary, this one is Billy (he touches each sheep on the forehead as he mentions its name).

Wolf: I'm not convinced that you are any better than the hired hand — and I am getting very hungry.

Shepherd: You can be as hungry as you like. But you may not harm these sheep. I am the Good Shepherd; I am ready to lay down my life for them rather than see them hurt by some old wolf!

Wolf: In that case, maybe I had better leave. I can go eat one of those other sheep I chased off.

Shepherd: Don't you dare touch any of those sheep! I have other sheep that do not belong to this flock. My Father wants them also to hear my voice and be led by me, so that there will be one flock and one shepherd!

Wolf: I'm so angry I could *growl*! (He lets out a loud growl and walks off dejectedly)

Narrator: And the wolf let out a terrible growl and walked off, never to return. And the sheep who had been scared away by the wolf returned one by one to join the flock of the Good Shepherd, for they knew they had found someone who would love them and never abandon them. (Pause) *The end.*

A BAPTISMAL MEDITATION

A Playlet for Baptism of the Lord Sunday
(Junior High Level)

Characters: Commentator
Father Bob, the priest
Sarah, the mother
Bill, the father
Uncle Ted, the godfather
Julie, the godmother
Rachael, the grandmother
Bill Senior, the grandfather
Fred, a friend

Setting: Characters form an arc on the altar steps facing the congregation. SARAH (holding a baby doll) and BILL stand in center on the highest step. Other relatives are spread out on either side. FR. BOB stands facing the baptismal group downstage right. Characters move from steps far downstage to area of the Communion rail when delivering their soliloquies.

Commentator: In the sacrament of Baptism, time and eternity cross in a way that can never be repeated in the life of the individual. But it also nourishes and strengthens the Christian community. In our Gospel playlet, we reflect on how Baptism might do this; it is called, "A Baptismal Meditation."

Father Bob: What do you ask of God's Church?

Sarah & Bill: We ask that our baby, John, might be baptized.

Father Bob: Are the godparents prepared to assist this child's parents in performing their duty as Christian parents?

Ted & Julie: We are.

Ted: (He steps away from the group) I'm Uncle Ted. For some reason I imagined there would be a lineup of screaming babies, all dressed in white. I didn't expect to be asked any questions. What do I think of all this? Humph! I think Johnny deserves the best godfather...whatever that involves. (He pauses) It's been such a long time since I was last in church. (He returns to group)

Father Bob: May the holy sacraments of baptism and confirmation preserve John as a faithful disciple and witness to your Gospel.

All: Lord hear us.

Rachael: I'm the grandmother. Yes, Lord, please hear our prayer. That's my girl, Sarah, standing there holding the baby. Things have changed a lot since Sarah was baptized — I wasn't even at the service in fact. But I did a lot of thinking and praying that afternoon in the hospital. That's why I so much wanted to be here today, so that I could say, "God help us all to help little Johnny grow to understand and love the meaning of this day." Yes, Lord, hear us!

Father Bob: Heavenly Father, you have called John to this birth in your Son so that by partaking in the faith of your Church he might receive everlasting life.

Fred: My name is Fred. I'm a friend. I thought this was going to be a party — mellow like the sunrise and we're all tied in a ring of love sort of ceremony. But the words they're saying won't leave it at that. I don't know what is going on here, but these words won't leave me alone.

Father Bob: Dearest parents and godparents: If your faith in Christ gives you the confidence to accept the role which the sacrament of Baptism bears with it, renew at this time the promises of your own Baptism. Affirm your faith in Christ Jesus, that same faith of Holy Mother Church in which John is about to be baptized.

Do you believe in God, the Father Almighty, Creator of heaven and earth?

All: We do.

Grandfather: My name is Bill, Senior. I am the grandfather. Here we are reciting the Creed again. I don't know about the others, but for me this is always kind of stirring. It's like an anthem that we Christians chorus up to God, generation after generation. Ancestors whose names I'll never know said it. Now we're saying it on behalf of little Johnny, 'til finally he'll be able to affirm it himself. God help us to help him reach this point.

Father Bob: Do you desire that your child, John, be baptized in the faith of the Church, whose creed we have proclaimed with you?

Parents and Godparents: We do. (Parents move down to Father Bob)

Father Bob: Then, John, I baptize you in the name of the Father and of the Son and of the Holy Spirit.

All: BLESSED BE GOD WHO CHOSE YOU IN CHRIST!

Bill: There is always so much distraction in an event such as this. I spent half the morning at delicatessens getting things ready for the reception.

Sarah: I was worried about the baby having a cold and fitting into the family's hand-me-down christening gown.

Bill: It's rather a jolt to realize that a Baptism isn't simply another viewer event with other characters. Everyone here is in this: God, the baby, John, and ourselves. We're the main characters and it's real.

Sarah: It's all so much all at once, that it's too much to absorb at one time. We can just repeat: "Blessed be God who chose you in Christ!"

Commentator: Every Baptism has the same text but a unique script. For the real event is more a dialogue of hearts than of prayers and actions. God touches everyone present in a unique way and the response returned is never exactly the same. It is on Baptism that our Christian community is built, and so today we acknowledge all those who have been baptised this past year, with their parents and families. To all of you we say, "Blessed be God who chose you in Christ!"
The end.

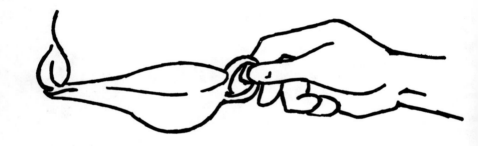

THE WISE AND FOOLISH YOUNG WOMEN

(Grades 6-8)

Characters: Narrator
Kate
Sally
Voices 1,2,3

Narrator: A story was once told by Jesus about some young women who were invited to act as lamp bearers for a big wedding. One of the young women we could call Kate.

Kate: Hello, that's me — casual Kate. I am not one to concern myself about things; I take them as they come. There is this big wedding with a party this evening. I just grab my shawl, grab my lamp, and I'm all set — no fuss, no bother.

Narrator: So, off went Kate to the wedding hall where she met Sally, another young woman who had been invited to be a lamp bearer.

Kate: Hello, Sally. My, don't you look dressed up this evening!

Sally: I'm so excited about the wedding. I've been working on my dress all week.

Kate:	Yes, I notice you have your lamp all shined up — looks like you're really set for this affair.
Narrator:	They sat with some of their other friends by the entrance to the hall and waited for the groom to show up. Finally, they fell asleep.
Voice 1:	Wake up, they are coming!
Voice 2:	Who?
Voice 3:	The groom, and his relatives too!
All:	Wake up, wake up, the groom and all his relatives are coming!
Kate:	What a lot of fuss people make about these things. (She is trimming her lamp)
Sally:	What an honor it will be to escort the groom into the wedding hall! (She also trims her lamp)
Kate:	Ah ... Sally, excuse me. This is kind of embarrassing, but my lamp just went out. Could I borrow some of your extra lamp oil?
Sally:	Gee, Kate ... if I lent you some of mine, I wouldn't have enough.
Voice 1:	Here they are!
Voice 2:	It's time to greet the groom!
Voice 3:	Hurry, Girls, go out and greet the groom, it's time!
Kate:	I'll go off and get some more oil at the store and catch up. No problem.
Narrator:	And so Sally went and lit the way of the groom and all his relatives as they made their way through the streets and into the wedding hall. By the time Kate got back, the doors of the hall were closed tight.
Kate:	I don't believe this! They've locked the doors! Hey in there, open up!
Voice:	Who is that out in the street shouting?
Kate:	It's me, Kate. I'm supposed to be at the party.

Voice: Sorry, ma'am, you must have the wrong address —
never heard of you.

Narrator: Now the moral of the story Jesus told is very
simple: "Keep your eyes open, for you know not
the day or the hour that I will come."
The end.

THE HOUSE OF GOD

**Week of Prayer for Christian Unity
(Primary Grades)**

Characters: Speaker 1
Speaker 2
Speaker 3
Speaker 4
Speaker 5
Speaker 6
Speaker 7
Speaker 8
Speaker 9
Speaker 10

Speaker 1:   There was once a house upon a hill
With doors on every side.
A signpost set before it read:
"Come in from far and wide.

It does not matter who you are
Or what distant roads you've trod.
This place is for you, for all in need:
This is the House of God."

Speaker 2:   But to the townsfolk at the foot of the hill,
God's House was way off too far.
They left it alone, and preferred to stay home
Behind doors they had locked and barred.

And should a stranger knock on their door
Or rap on their window pane,
They would raise a great shout, which would
echo without
Whose message was always the same:

Speakers 3,4,5: "I've got what I've got, and I'll keep what
I have
Regardless of what you do.
Stay away from my home and leave me alone,
There's nothing in here for you!"

Speaker 6: So it had been for year after year
It seemed thus it would always remain.
You could plead, you could beg,
You could weep, you could rave,
You would still hear the same refrain:

3,4,5: "I've got what I've got, and I'll keep what
I have
Regardless of what you do.
Stay away from my home and leave me alone
There's nothing in here for you!"

Speaker 7: Until one black and stormy night
The breath of God's spirit burst forth.
It ripped open the shutters of each of their homes
And knocked down the strongest of doors.

The wind drove the townsfolk to the top of the hill
'Til before them God's house they saw.
Then the light within beckoned them in,
And they entered with fear and awe.

Speaker 8: They found themselves in a beautiful hall
Resplendent with golden rays
And to their surprise — already inside —
Were all those they had turned away.
There were sick, there were poor, the tired
and weak, the beggars, the sinners, the lame.
Yet all fitted in, each had a place
And everyone was treated the same.

Speaker 9: At this sight, the townsfolk (who had just entered
in)
Felt no longer afraid.
They forgot all their fears and dried all their tears
And decided they wanted to stay.

In this lovely place, they felt right at home
It was just like their own but more:
There was warmth, there was care,
There was food all could share — (Pause)
Then they noticed *there weren't any doors!*

3,4,5: "This will not do," they said with dismay,
"We can abide these sick and these poor,
But this could be the best home we have known,
If somehow we could close up the doors!"

Speaker 10: Then they all set about, to shut others out
To barricade each entrance and stair.
To close up the hall, by building new walls
Of furniture, tables and chairs.

And then once more God's Spirit moved,
And burst open every door,
And drove the townsfolk from the hall
With a mighty wind and roar.

"God's house is open to all, my friends,"
The Spirit's voice did say:
"Go back to your homes and open your doors,
And *never* turn others away.

"Be kind to the poor and help the weak
Take in travelers from the cold.
Open your shutters, let your light shine forth,
Help the sick and the old.

"And if this is done, though some may scoff,
And others think it odd,
Then you will be welcomed back again,
When *your* house is like the House of God."
The end.

Note: The poem can be recited by a number of students, either in chorus or individually, using various microphones. The central action (beggars coming to the door, townsfolk being driven from their homes, etc.) might also be pantomimed.

THE WORD OF THE LORD

Scripture Service
(Junior High)

Characters: **Bishop:** An intelligent leader, capable of flashes of oratory, but easily attracted to wealth and power. He is dressed in a chasuble (such as the priest wears at Mass) over a long white inner garment with sleeves (the alb). On his head he wears a miter, he carries a shepherd's staff and wears a stole over the chasuble. He might also wear a gold pendant from his neck.

Dame Charming: A wealthy talkative person. She wears rich gowns, jewels, and has an elaborate hair piece.

Sister Pius: A straight-laced, strict person, and her clothes show it. While her clothes show no signs of poverty, the color is dark and the style severe. She is not exactly a nun, but might wear some sort of simple veil.

Bailiff Brown: A strong, at times rough police officer. He wears a suit of armor or at least a metal chest piece, and carries an ax in his hand. His clothing can show some signs of wealth.

Merchant Mark: A large, none too intelligent

tradesman. He is also wealthy and shows it in his clothes.

Samuel Simpson: A lean-looking, scholarly type. His clothes are very simple but in bright colors.

Peasant Peter: Wears a rough peasant tunic, perhaps with a hooded cape for cold weather.

Peasant Polly: The same as Peasant Peter.

Father Robert: Wears a long black gown, with a simple stole over it. In Scene 3 he also wears a very expensive chasuble.

Narrator

Soldier: One of Bailiff Brown's men
(Not a speaking part).

A Second Soldier

Setting: The action of the play takes place in the sanctuary. In the original staging, titles were shown as slides on a screen located to the side of the altar. If this is not convenient, scene titles could be incorporated into the narrator's lines. As the playlet begins, a slide is shown which reads, "The Word of the Lord." Actors take their positions in a tableaux before the altar.

Narrator: I would like to tell you about the Word of the Lord, but what we see before us is no help at all. *Such* a pious congregation! Look at the devout priest. Even the holy bishop is present! All are at peace with one another. Human frailty and selfishness, hatred and foolishness, have been left at the door. But where is the book of Scripture, the Word of the Lord?

It is not there ... and for a *reason*. If there ever were in real life such a perfect Christian community as this, one so good that it had only to *honor* and not to *listen* to God's Word, then it would have no need for the book of Scripture.

If I am to tell you about the Word of the Lord and its meaning, we must turn away from this dream-like setting to a *living* Church, peopled by weak but well-meaning human beings as ourselves.

(Slide: "Persecution: 250 A.D.")

Narrator: The year is 250 A.D. The world is at peace. Our little community has at last felt secure enough to build its own Church building. Then, unexpectedly, the Chief of Government decides to act.

Mark: What's happening? Why has the Mass stopped?

Samuel: Bailiff Brown and the police have just come into the Church. Bailiff Brown is going to speak.

Brown: All right everyone, quiet down, quiet down! I've got an order here from the Chief of Government and I don't want any trouble. Right now, we're all going to go down to City Hall, line up in front of the statue of the Chief, and put three beads of incense on the fire in front of the statue. That goes for everyone!

Samuel: Bailiff Brown, you are one of us, a Christian yourself. You know we can't offer sacrifice!

Peter: But where has the bishop gone? He ran out the back door when the bailiff came in.

Brown: Just three grains of incense to the statue of the Chief and no one will get hurt. It'll be all over in a wink. I'm just doing my job, folks, doing my job.

(Slide: "Two days later")
There is a short period of silence here. The screen then goes black and action resumes.

Sister Pius: (In a state of shock) I never would have believed it possible.

Charming: Disgusting, I say. The bishop just got up and ran away.

Sister Pius: I wasn't here when it happened, but I would like to know if anyone offered incense at City Hall.

Charming: I simply can't say. I wasn't here either. Here comes Peasant Peter, perhaps he knows.

Sister Pius: Peasant Peter, you were here on Sunday when it happened, weren't you?

Peter: No. I was on the road coming here when Bailiff Brown arrived. But look here comes the rest of the community — at least most of us — why, there is even the Bishop!

Charming: Why of all the nerve — how dare he show his face among us?

Polly: (speaking with great sorrow) They won't give us the bodies. After the executions they wouldn't allow us to have them. They buried them in the trash dump. Bailiff Brown and his men are on guard there still.

Sister Pius: Executions? Bodies? What are you saying?

Bishop: Brothers and sisters, please listen. We are here to celebrate not the death but the birth of three of our members into God's heavenly Kingdom. We are blessed for the three martyrs who would not worship a false god: Father Robert, Merchant Mark, Samuel Simpson, pray for us!

Charming: How can that man speak after running away. Shame!

Bishop: Others amongst us, myself, first of all, have failed. We have been weak and cowardly and for this we ask God's forgiveness and your pardon.

Sister Pius: (angrily) That's fine for you to say, Bishop, "forgive and forget," but that's not good enough for me!

Charming: God's Church has no room for runaways and traitors. What does the community say?

Polly: Hold your tongue! There were more of us than the bishop who fled or offered sacrifice.

Sister Pius: Well, I am with Dame Charming, and I will have nothing to do with any of you!

Bishop: Brethren, let us humbly bow heads and listen to God's Word.

(A very brief pause, then, as if reading) "And they came to Jesus and said, Lord, teach us how to pray, and He said, you should pray like this: 'Our Father forgive us our trespasses as we forgive those who trespass against us and deliver us from every evil.' And then Jesus said, 'If you forgive others their failings, your Heavenly Father will also forgive you.' "

Charming: I will not forgive you, Bishop. You have defiled the Church. I will leave!

Bishop: (Finishing the reading) This is the Word of the Lord.

All: (except Dame Charming — said slowly and sadly) Thanks be to God.

Narrator: (beginning immediately, with the final slide projected) And the small community was broken. Some would not accept the Lord's Word that "he came to call sinners as well as the just."

Then time passed — hundreds of years. The great Empire collapsed, learning died out.

(Slide: "Hard Times: 800 A.D.")

Narrator: It is now 800 A.D. The cast of characters is the same, for though the world changes people are always basically the same. Things now are different from before. Hard times have arrived, and the candle of faith burns very dimly indeed.

Fr. Robert: Why are you here?

Peter: Father Robert, you know why we are here. It is the Lord's day. Will there be the Liturgy of the Word and the Bread?

Fr. Robert　　(wearily) It is a very cold Sunday, and none of you have paid a tithe to the Church.

Polly:　　But Father, we have walked for miles through the mud and wet to come here.

Fr. Robert　　And I am sick. You people wish me to serve and lead you. It has been one hundred years since the roof has been fixed. The snow blows through the windows.

Sister Pius:　　But the times are black, Father Robert. A barbarian tribe is roaming through the valley. We are starving and hungry.

Fr. Robert:　　But where is everyone else? Where is Bailiff Brown and the Bishop; where is Merchant Mark and Dame Charming? I'll tell you. They are in the castle on the hill where it is safe, and if I had any sense, I would be there too! Leave me, I am not feeling well.

Peter:　　Then there will be no Mass?

Polly:　　(brightly) I have an idea, everyone! Since there will be no Mass, let us take oak leaves and make wreathes and go in procession to the fountain spring of Venusia!

Fr. Robert:　　The what?

Peter:　　The spring, with the magic water!

Polly:　　Yes, Father, you wash in the spring with a spider web and a frog's foot in your left hand. It brings good luck!

Fr. Robert:　　(kindly but firmly) Yes, yes, but you know I forbid such things.

Sister Pius:　　You forbid such things, Father Robert, and we obey you, but you will not lead us in the Liturgy of the Word and Bread.

Fr. Robert:　　All right, my children: I am sick and cold, the roof leaks, but we shall celebrate Mass today. (A short pause) "This is the Word of the Lord. Then fixing his eyes on his disciples, Jesus said, 'How happy are you who are hungry now; you shall be satisfied. Happy are you who weep now; you shall laugh. Happy are you when people hate you, drive you out on account of the Son of God ... your reward will be great in heaven'

(Solemnly) This is the Word of the Lord!"

Peter, Polly, Pius: (together, joyfully) Thanks be to God!

Polly: Thank you, Father Robert, the sun will shine again, you'll see!

Narrator: (begins reading immediately) Yet somehow through a period of bleakness, when people could barely read, God's word was kept alive in men and women; their hearts, and their faith were sustained until, with the passing of centuries, the "sun did shine" on Christianity once again.

(Slide: The Age of Faith: 1200 A.D.)

It is the year 1200 A.D. The Church is at the center of arts, culture, and politics. Some call it the age of faith, for on the surface it seems as if for the first time, *God's Word* and the *world's word* have become one and the same. But there are always those who know that the two can never be the same, and who speak out.

Charming: The bishop will be here today to see the new art work behind the high altar. (Stumbling into Samuel Simpson) Oops! Samuel Simpson, what are you doing up here in front?

Samuel: (praying) Lord, make me an instrument of your peace, where there is darkness, let me bring your light.

Charming: Now, Samuel, you are not going to insist on being in the wrong seat again, not with the bishop here this morning. This is my pew. I donated it to the Church. Now you just go to the back of the Church with the other peasants.

Brown and
Mark: Good morning, Dame Charming!

Charming: Good morning, Bailiff Brown and Merchant Mark. It is so nice to have you back here among us.

Brown: Why yes, I notice that even Sister Pius is here. Splendidly glorious Sunday. With the Lord Bishop coming, things couldn't be better! Samuel, what are you doing up here? These seats are in the first class section!

Samuel: Lord, make me an instrument of your peace ...

Mark: Good boy, say your prayers. But no talk about the poor and starving this morning; is that clear, Samuel?

Charming: Good morning, Father Robert. You look very elegant in those new robes Merchant Mark donated to the Church.

Fr. Robert: Yes, yes, thank you all. Oops! (He has bumped into Samuel) Samuel Simpson, you know you are not in your proper place. Go to the back, the Bishop is arriving ... and I want no talk from you about your poor and starving that we are neglecting. No talk, you hear, or I'll have Bailiff Brown throw you out in the street.

Charming: My word, Samuel still has not moved after all that. I'm sure the Lord Bishop will put him in his place! Here he comes now.

Bishop: Reverend Father Robert, Lord Bailiff Brown, Noble Dame Charming, Merchants, and peasants of the community. Before I read the good news of the Gospel, I have some other good news to share with you. One of your members has petitioned the Lord Holy Father in Rome for official permission to preach poverty and take care of the poor. It is a Godly request, something which you and I could all stand to do more of, and I, as Bishop, have supported this request. Samuel Simpson, the Holy Father grants your requests and sends, you his blessing. (A very short pause) Let us bow our heads now and listen to the Word of the Lord:

"And Jesus said to them, Do not store up treasures here on earth for yourselves, where moths destroy and thieves break in and steal. But store up treasures for yourselves in heaven. Where your treasure is, there will your heart be also."

Charming: (quietly) Where did he find that passage of Scripture?

Bishop: This is the Word of the Lord!

Peter and Polly: Thanks be to God!

Mark: (grumbling to himself) Samuel Simpson is no more than a common pest.

Bishop: (growing angry) Brothers and sisters, though it grieves us and disturbs us from our set and comfortable ways, let us acknowledge God's message just read. (firmly) *This is the Word of the Lord!*

All: (happily) Thanks be to God ...

Narrator: But though the word of the Lord is constantly proclaimed, there are always those who shut it out from their hearing. No one is excepted from this, not even those whose duty it is to lead the Christian community.

(Slide: "Threat from Within: 1600 A.D.")

Narrator: The year is 1600 A.D. Europe is swept by religious controversy. The Word of the Lord which has so long held the community together now has become a source of division. Confusion rules.

Sister Pius: (rapidly and loudly) Revelation, revolution, rip out the roots, turn over the soil. I have heard the Word of the Lord, heed me!

On verse 36, chapter 36 of the book of the prophet, the Lord declares that he who doth not leave his father and mother, wife and children ...

Mark: Listen to Sister Pius. She has been inspired, she speaks the truth!

Polly: It's the rage, you know. It's sweeping the country. The old Church is dead!

Brown:	Yes, the old Bible was wrong. We've got new translations now, everything is up-to-date!
Peter:	But what does Father Robert say?
Samuel:	He's not saying anything!
Peter:	But what does the Bishop say?
Charming:	Oh, he's off hunting as usual or visiting his rich friends in the country!
Sister Pius:	Reformation, deformation, burn down the old, raise up the new!
Samuel:	The King himself has crossed over! And I have seen Bailiff Brown preaching in the town square from the steps of City Hall!
Sister Pius:	(wildly) On verse 36 of book 36 in the Prophet of Chapter it says clearly that ...
Peter:	Father Robert, have you nothing to say?
	(There is a moment of silence, and then)
Fr. Robert:	I say that I am confused and afraid. But this I know. What Sister Pius preaches is not the faith our fathers have handed down to us. It is not the creed we profess, nor the sacraments we celebrate.
Charming:	Why, that's just the same old hash re-hashed. But wait! (A brief pause) Who is that man who has just entered the Church?
Polly:	My word! — Isn't he the Bishop?
Brown:	Hey, Lord Bishop; where are your hunting dogs and white horses?
Bishop:	(meekly) I sold them.
All:	*You what!!*
Bishop:	(quietly, after a brief pause) I sold my horses and hunting dogs. I sold them all... Dearly beloved, listen. Unworthy though I be, as poor an example as I have been, the truth which I

proclaim is that which our fathers have handed down, lived, and died for. I have been appointed by God to exercise the office of pastor and leader. I have failed — may God forgive me. But today, let me begin anew and proclaim the authentic faith of the Church. I will begin with the Gospel. (pause) "And Jesus said to them: 'Anyone who welcomes a little child welcomes me. But if anyone scandalizes one of these little ones, it would be better if he were drowned in the sea with a great millstone around his neck.' " This is the Word of the Lord!

All: (slowly) Thanks be to God.

Narrator: The little community of the Church has its leaders and members, each with a proper role to play and the duty to help one another listen and respond as we should.

(Slide: "Another Time, Another Place")

Narrator: The story of God's Word is always the same — for though times and problems change, people remain basically the same. It is the year 2000. Who knows what trials our own Christian community will have to face?

Fr. Robert: Today we will not read the Gospel of the Lord. In its place I wish to discuss ...

Mark: What in the world is he talking about?

Peter: He is very educated and clever ...

Fr. Robert: and speak of an idea which I thought you might find interesting.

Charming: (excitedly) Oh yes, isn't he magnificent!

Fr. Robert: About the relationship of philosophy to anxiety ...

Mark: What in the world is he talking about?

Peter: He has a brilliant mind ...

Fr. Robert: The ancients believed that the spots on the moon emitted certain rays ...

Polly:	(nervously) This is the Holy Gospel ...
Fr. Robert:	And as Professor Von Romberg ...
Peter and Polly:	And they came to Jesus and said: Lord teach us how to pray ...
Fr. Robert:	As I was saying: Von Romberg, in his book on metaphysical symmetry ...
Brown, Polly, Peter, Samuel:	"And Jesus said, 'You should pray like this: Our Father, who art in heaven, hallowed be ...
Fr. Robert:	Excuse me, everyone! What is the meaning of this?
Polly:	We want to hear the Word of God, Father Robert, not *your* word.
All:	"Thy kingdom come, Thy will be done, on earth as it is in heaven ..."
Fr. Robert:	But it is so simple, and you have heard it so many times before ...
Peter:	And that is why we have come.
All:	(shouting) Hear! Hear!
Fr. Robert:	All right, all right. (pause) Let us bow our heads and listen to the good news of Jesus Christ. "And they came to Jesus and said, 'Lord, why do you speak in parables?' And Jesus replied (his voice trails off interrupted by music) ...
Narrator:	Our playlet concludes here, but the story continues. For God's Word is not something the Church has been given merely to honor. We have received it that our lives might be inspired and renewed. Until time turns into the fullness of eternity, the Christian community will find healing and strength in the Word of the Lord. (Pause) *The end.*
Note:	Because of its length, the playlet might more easily be performed as a dramatic reading.

HEAVEN'S WAY

Lent
(Primary Grades)

Parts: James
John
Six Readers

Setting: Two microphones are used. JAMES and JOHN stand together at left microphone, the SIX READERS stand at right in a small cluster. If preparation time permits, parts should be memorized.

Reader #1: "Heaven's Way"

James: "John come along, the master calls!"
James told his friend one day.
"He's asking us to go with him,
Up the mountainside to pray."

Reader #1: The slope was steep, the winds blew free
With vistas spreading wide.

James: "What a great place for a picnic," said James
"Close by the good Lord's side."

Reader #2: Jesus climbed on far ahead,
With James and John behind.

James: "Hurry" said James, "if we can keep up with him
Who knows what we will find?"

John: "I'm nervous, James," John shouted back
"This is more than simple prayer
Alone with Jesus on a mountain top,
Who knows what awaits us there?"

Reader #2: Higher up the trail they went
Above where eagles fly
Beyond a rainbow's arching rays
Past clouds that towered high.

James: "Jesus, wait!" James shouted out
"It's time we took a rest. (Pause)
But who is that you're walking with
Upon the mountain crest?"

John: And then John said in a hush-filled tone
As he felt his skin grow cold:
"He's walking with the angels, and
With prophets from of old.

"Behold his face, see how it shines
This is sacred ground we've trod.
The Lord Jesus is wrapped in prayer,
He's talking to his God."

Reader #3: Small animals looked up in awe,
The birds, the grass stood still
The Son of Man was bent in prayer
To hear his Father's will.

James: John knelt in fear and trembling,
But James made bold to say,
"Lord, don't stop, go higher still,
We're with you all the way!

"Let's leave these crags and brambles
Forget this world of sin,
Let's soar past skies and moons and suns,
Let eternity begin!

"No more dusty roads and hungry nights,
No more cripples, sick or poor,
We've reached the threshold of the stars,
There's paradise in store."

Reader #4:   But they didn't go to heaven
Not that afternoon.
They didn't fly on angels wings
Or soar up past the moon.

Instead (Pause) Jesus turned and walked away,
Down the rocky slope
To do again his Father's work,
Sharing love and faith and hope.

Reader #5:   Until one Friday afternoon
To another hill he came
A place of grief and agony called
Calvary by name.

It was not a time of glory,
There was no music from on high
There were no colored rainbows,
Or starbursts in the sky.

James: Nor was there a James that shouted:
"Jesus, we're with you all the way!"

John: In fact, all his friends had left him.
(Pause)
Only John remained to pray.

Reader #6:   (slowly) And there they hung him on a tree
Amidst the weak and poor.
It was on *that* hill that Jesus
Was claimed by God, (Pause)
And opened heaven's door.
(Pause) *The end.*

SOMETIMES IT CAUSES ME TO TREMBLE

Lenten Prayer/Reconciliation Service
(Junior High Level)

Synopsis: This is a dramatized examination of conscience involving Scripture readings, dramatic recitation, and slides. It is intended for Junior High students and would form a part of a group Penance Service.

Reading parts: First Reader
Second Reader
Third Reader
Fourth Reader
Narrator
Jesus
Peter
Pilate (if necessary, Peter and Pilate could be

Slide played by the same person)

Descriptions: Slides of student art work are not strictly necessary. They do, however, help focus the attention of the congregation.

1. Christ on the cross
2. Title Slide, *"Sometimes it causes me to tremble"*
3. Christ washes Peter's feet at the Last Supper
4. Christ prays while his apostles sleep in the garden
5. Christ before the Roman Procurator, Pontius Pilate
6. Christ dies on the cross
7. Christ on the cross

Lighting: All houselights are kept off throughout the dra-
                    matic presentation. A copy of the script should be
                    provided for the student in charge of lighting, to
                    avoid any delays at the end of the performance.

**Speaking
Arrangements:** Unless there are two microphones available, all
                    parts are read from the pulpit. If a second mic-
                    rophone can be used (or if actors have loud voices),
                    first and second readers read at pulpit, others
                    speak from opposite side of the sanctuary.

At the beginning of the presentation all house lights go off.
Flashlights or small desk lights are used by readers.

Slides 1 & 2 *are projected on a screen placed at the side of the altar.*

Slide *off.*

1st Reader: Dear Jesus, what were you thinking about on the
                    night before you died? You knew you were in
                    trouble — what did *you* do?
                    I would have been on my way out of town. Better
                    still, I wouldn't have got into trouble to begin with.
                    There are two basic principles I follow: "Don't
                    make waves," and if I do: "Every man for him-
                    self!" I'm a *careful* Christian. Someone in my class
                    is hurt, I leave him (her) alone. The hurt will pass
                    in time. Someone needs help at home? I mind my
                    own business. Mom and Dad will get on me if they
                    think it's important enough. A friend of mine is
                    doing something wrong? I keep me mouth shut.
                    That's his (her) business. This is what I mean by
                    being a *careful* Christian. I don't hurt other people
                    and I watch out for myself. Do I really believe this
                    is right — deep down in my heart? I think I do —
                    and I think, Jesus, you would understand. But I
                    could be wrong. What did you do, Lord, when you
                    knew you were in trouble? What were you thinking
                    about on the night before *you* died?

Slide 3 *flashes simultaneously on the screen, as narrator reads.*

Narrator: And so Jesus rose from the table and set down his cloak; then he girded himself with a towel and pouring water into a basin began to wash the feet of his disciples. Then he dried them with the towel. When he came to Simon Peter, however, Peter said to him:

Peter: Lord, I will not allow you to wash my feet!

Jesus: If I do not wash your feet, you will never share with me the kingdom of heaven.

Peter: Lord, then wash not only my feet, but my hands and my head also!

Narrator: Then when he had finished, Jesus explained to them:

Jesus: You call me teacher, and that I am. If I whom you know as teacher and Lord wash the feet of others, then you too must be ready to wash the feet of one another.

Slide *off.*

2nd Reader: Dear Lord, what did you do before you died? Did you have time to pray? I pray sometimes — when I'm alone. I pray in emergencies. But *every day*? Who needs it and who has time?

I know you are out there, Lord, and I know some people pray everyday. But these are old people or little kids. After all, it's what you *do* not what you *say* that counts! For myself, I'm too busy during the day and too tired at night. Though to be honest, I sometimes feel like I'm drying up inside — and sometimes at Church in the pause after the priest says, "Let us pray," I wonder if I still know how to speak to you at all.

When I am older, perhaps, things will change — there's no time now. Lord, did you have time to pray when you were busy with important things?

Slide 4 *appears on screen as narrator reads.*

Narrator: Then, when supper had finished, Jesus and a few of his disciples went to an olive grove named Gethsemani. There he told his disciples:

Jesus: Sit here while I go and pray.

Narrator: Taking Peter, James, and John along with him, Jesus began to be filled with fear and anguish. He said to them:

Jesus: My soul is sad even unto death: stay here and watch with me.

Narrator: Going a little bit forward, he fell upon the ground in prayer and said: "My Father, if it is possible let this cup of suffering pass from me, yet not my will but thine be done."

When he returned, he found his disciples asleep once more.

Jesus: Can't you stay awake for at least an hour. Pray that you do not fall into temptation.

Slide *off.*

3rd Reader: Dear Jesus, did you ever tell the truth when it practically caused you to be killed? Honesty may have worked in the old days, but not anymore. Oh, I'm normally truthful. Honesty is the best policy, you know. But not when it hurts.

If I am caught doing something wrong, I just make up a story. I am very good at it. Besides, some adults and teachers are so used to being lied to by kids my age, they don't really expect more. After all, who does it hurt?

Not everyone feels this way, of course. A priest once told me that every sin is just a kind of lie, and if my words aren't true, soon my actions won't be true either. As I see it, however, lying is just a bad habit.

Jesus, perhaps *you* could tell me something: would you have told the truth if it practically caused you to be killed?

Slide 5 *appears on screen as narrator reads.*

Narrator: Jesus was brought to the Roman Procurator, Pontius Pilate. Pilate said to him:

Pilate: Are you the king of the Jews?

Jesus: My kingdom is not of this world.

Pilate: But are you a king?

Jesus: You are the one who says I am king. The reason I was born and the reason why I came into the world was to bear witness to the truth. Any person who believes in the truth hears my voice.

Narrator: And Pilate answered:

Pilate: *Truth?* What is truth?

Slide *off.*

4th Reader: (no pause) Dear Lord, were you lonely on that last day? Sometimes I think to be alone is the very worst thing that can happen to a person. It is to *me*. To be left standing on the side while others are talking and laughing. To walk into a room and be ignored — to ask questions and not be answered. I would rather do anything than have such things happen to me. A teacher once told me: "Be an engine, not a caboose." That's only asking for trouble in my opinion. Following the crowd is better. I laugh when my friends laugh; if they are making fun of someone, so do I. Otherwise I'm afraid I'll be left out — left alone.

Is this right? I really don't know. Perhaps, dear Lord, you could answer that question for me. Did you ever experience what it's like to be left alone and abandoned?

Slide 6 *appears on screen as narrator reads.*

Narrator: Pilate said to the crowd:

Pilate: Do you desire that I release to you the king of the Jews?

Narrator: The crowd shouted back: "Crucify him!" In order
                       to satisfy the crowd, Pilate then had Jesus whipped
                       and given over to be crucified.

                       It was about nine in the morning when Jesus was
                       hung on the cross. Those passing by mocked him
                       saying: "Why don't you save yourself and come
                       down from the cross!" The chief priests and scribes
                       insulted him, shouting: "He saved other people,
                       but look, he cannot save himself!" The men who
                       were crucified with him likewise made fun of him.

                       Finally when noon came, darkness fell across the
                       land, and Jesus said:

Jesus: It ... is ... finished.

                       And bowing his head, he gave up his spirit.

Slide 7 *appears on screen for several seconds.*

Slide *off* — **House Lights** *on.*
The end.

HILDA'S DREAM

A Playlet for the Feast of the Immaculate Conception
(Middle Grades)

Characters: Announcer
Hilda, an elderly woman
Matilda, an elderly woman (**M**)
Harvey, an elderly man (**H**)
Statue 1: Julius Caesar
Statue 2: William Shakespeare
Statue 3: Amelia Johnson
Statue 4: the Virgin Mary

Setting: After introduction by ANNOUNCER, STATUES stand in frozen positions across top of altar platform. HILDA, MATILDA, and HARVEY stand in a cluster to the right of statues on the level of the sanctuary. Announcer speaks from pulpit.

Announcer: The name of our Gospel playlet is Hilda's Dream. Hilda was an old woman. She loved God very much and went to Church every day. But when the feasts of Mary came by she always turned grumpy.

Hilda: My name is Hilda. Ordinarily I am a rather sweet old lady. But when a feast day of Mary comes near, I become an old grouch. That is, until lately.

Announcer: You see, the night before the feast, Hilda had this strange dream. Instead of being in church, she was

in what seemed like a museum together with her
two friends, Harvey and Matilda. They were *all*
grumpy.

Hilda: Matilda and Harvey, old friends, this is a strange
museum. I think all these old, dusty statues can
talk.

M. and H.:   Hilda, my dear. It's all so *dull.* They're old and cold
and long, long gone.

Statue 1:   Now, just a minute, you three. I'm Julius Caesar,
so perk up! Travel back in your imaginations to the
glory of Rome. Think of my great armies, of the
battles I won. There is *no reason* why you should be
grumpy.

Hilda: Yes there is, Julius. You just make me feel *ancient.*
Whatever you were is long, long gone.

M. and H.:   That's right, Julius. You're old and cold and long,
long gone.

Statue 2:   I heard what you just said to old Julius and think
you have a point.

Matilda: Hilda, Harvey, who is talking now?

Statue 2:   My name is William Shakespeare. I wrote better
plays and poems than anyone in the English lan-
guage. My stories have made millions of people
laugh and cry. Thinking of me and what human
genius can do should cheer you up!

Hilda: Yes, William, when I was young and full of life,
you did make me laugh and cry with your stories.
But now I am old and I don't want any more
stories.

M. and H.:   You're no fun to us anymore, William. You're old
and cold and long, long gone.

Statue 3:   Enough of that gloom, you three. My name is
Amelia Johnson. I was the greatest woman athlete
of all time. I ran faster, jumped higher, won more
gold medals than anyone. Thinking of me and
what the human body can do should cheer you up!

Hilda: Amelia, when I was young and could dream of what I might become someday, you inspired me. But now you just remind me of how little I can do.

Matilda: You don't mean anything to us now, Amelia.

Harvey: You are old and cold and long, long gone. (Pause) There is one more statue left, Hilda and Matilda. What will it say?

Statue 4: Hello. My name is Mary; I am the mother of Jesus.

Statue 1: Who? I never heard of you. You don't belong here — you never won any battles.

Statue 2: You certainly don't rank with me. How many plays did you write?

Statue 3: I have the record for the fastest mile. Mary, you don't seem to fit in with us.

Statue 4: I led a simple life in the service of my Lord and neighbor.

Matilda: Mary, we really would like to tell you how old and cold and long, long gone you are. But somehow, now that the statues mention it, you *don't* fit in here.

Mary: Of course not, Matilda. I am not something past, who has no relationship to you. What I am now is what my Son Jesus calls you to be: a person made whole and holy in God's love.

Hilda: But we are so old and useless.

Mary: There is no age in God's love, Hilda. Just completion.

Harvey: But you were specially chosen, Mary.

Mary: No, Harvey, all of us were chosen. In a way I was just the first. Perhaps I really shouldn't be left on a pedestal with the other statues. I am not a sign of what a human being once did, but of the blessedness that God calls all of us to be — for all generations, a sign of hope for all those who feel weak and abandoned.

(Characters freeze in place, except for Hilda, who moves to the center and looks upward toward the church entrance)

Announcer: And with that, Hilda woke up from her strange dream. At first she thought it was *just* a dream and nothing else. Then she wondered if the feast days of Mary made her grumpy because she *had* treated Mary as someone that had no relation to her, someone cold and gone, rather than a sign of the wonders that God has done and will do for all his children. (Pause) *The end.*

HURTING AND HOPING

**Graduation/Commencement Prayer Service
(Grades 8-9)**

Parts: (Actors, other than Maggie, play several characters each)
Maggie
Left Reader 1 (girl's part)
Left Reader 2 (boy's part)
Left Reader 3 (girl's part)
Right Reader 1 (boy's part)
Right Reader 2 (girl's part)
Right Reader 3 (boy's part)

Setting: All parts are read from script. MAGGIE stands at front center beneath a spotlight, other readers stand at left and right (indicated by 'L' and 'R') also spotlighted. Script is read at a brisk pace with the exception of the meditation sequences at the end of each scene.

Maggie: Up in the morning: hello Mom; hello Dad.

L. Reader 1: Your blouse is dirty, Maggie.

R. Reader 1: Doesn't my daughter own anything but jeans?

Maggie: Walk to school; sun is shining; blossoms on the trees.

L. Reader 3: Hi, Maggie!

The Golden Link

Maggie: Hi, Jill.

L. Reader 3: Maggie, look at Sandra coming up the street. Who is *that* she's walking with?

R. Reader 3: Anybody got a smoke?

Maggie: Up in the morning, walk to school, blossoms on the trees.

L. Reader 2: Maggie, your last essay was *so* good. What happened to this one?

L. Reader 1: (Imitating a loud speaker announcement) Today third period will be shortened by a half-hour, and second period will be shortened by fifteen minutes except for those reporting to driver's education in the girl's gym, which will not be shortened by half an hour.

L. Reader 2: Maggie, could you loan me some money for lunch?

R. Reader 2: (whispering loudly) What answer did you get for number nine?

Maggie: School's out; walk home; wind blowing (she turns on noisey radio music from a recorder set on a chair in front of her).

L. Reader 1: Maggie, *turn that noise off!*

Maggie: Mom, I'm doing my *homework* (she turns music off).

R. Reader 1: Good evening, Maggie, what happened at school today? (he does not wait for an answer) Busy time at the office. I think we're going to land that contract after all. (he rambles on) You know, we got this new 3M copier, does both sides and color, really something ...

Maggie: (interrupting her father) Good night, Mom.

L. Reader 1: 'Night, Maggie.

Maggie: Good night, Dad.

R. Reader 2: Good night, dear. Er ... don't let the bed bugs bite!

(There is a brief pause, the mood shifts, then Maggie speaks)

Maggie: Dear God, I know people care about me. But if only they'd stop long enough to listen to me, or smile, or ask how I feel. But there is always tomorrow, next week, or next year. (she rattles off the remainder of her prayer mechanically) Help me to be a good Christian. Help me to love you forever. Amen.

(There is a pause, then the action resumes at a brisk pace)

Maggie: Up in the morning: hello, Mom; hello, Dad!

L. Reader 1: Maggie, did you hear that your grandmother died earlier this morning?

Maggie: (stunned) *Grandma?*

R. Reader 1: You'll have to go to school today. Your Mom and I will be busy until late this afternoon making the funeral arrangements.

Maggie: Walk to school; sky is cloudy; rain in the air.

L. Reader 3: Morning, Maggie. Did you see Rip Torn on television last night — *it was wild!*

Maggie: (in a hollow voice) My grandmother died this morning.

L. Reader 3: Too bad. (brief pause) Who is that over there talking with Sandra?

L. Reader 2: Maggie, would you please stop staring out the window while I'm speaking to the class. What's the matter with you today?

R. Reader 3: What's wrong with Maggie?

R. Reader 2: Oh, her uncle or grandmother or somebody died.

R. Reader 3: The way she's acting, you'd think it was somebody in her family or something.

R. Reader 1: There will be no driver's training in the gym...

Maggie: Walk home, sky is black, rain puddles on the ground. (a brief pause) Hello, Sandra. Yes, this is

	Maggie. I've been trying to get you on the phone all afternoon. You heard about my grandmother? (pause) Oh, you'd rather not talk about it. I was hoping I could share — No ... (pause) No ... I don't think I'll want to go the rock concert this weekend.
L. & R.	
Reader 1:	Good night, Maggie.
Maggie:	Good night, Mom; good night, Dad.
	(There is a pause to allow the mood to shift, then Maggie speaks)
Maggie:	Dear God: it seems sometimes as if all life were business, arrangements to be made, places to go. Today there was no place for grandma's death — or sadness or prayer. Dear God, help me to understand people and life — but also death, too. (mechanically, but somewhat more thoughtfully than in the first scene) Help me to be a good Christian. Help me to love you forever. Amen.
	(There is a pause, then the action resumes at a brisk pace)
Maggie:	Up in the morning, off to school, sun is shining.
R. Reader 2:	Maggie, that's a cute dress you're wearing.
Maggie:	Thank you!
L. Reader 3:	Maggie, who was that I saw you with yesterday during the ten minute break?
Maggie:	Oh, just a boy I met.
L. Reader 2:	Maggie, would you stop staring out the window and pay attention to today's lesson.
Maggie:	I'm sorry, Mr. Brown.
L. Reader 1:	I'd like to announce that the third period today will be interrupted by the second, so that ...
Maggie:	(excitedly) Sandra, are you going to the dance tonight?
R. Reader 2:	Are you?
Maggie:	Jim asked me if I would.

R. Reader 2: Who is *Jim*?

Maggie: Oh, just a boy I met yesterday. (pause)
Go home; walking on clouds.

L. Reader 1: Maggie, are you feeling all right? You've hardly touched your dinner this evening.

R. Reader 1: What kind of boy is this Jim? Do we know his parents?

Maggie: I'm so excited, Mom. How do I look?

R. Reader 1: If you ask me, this Jim fellow better hurry up or you're not going to get to the dance on time.

Maggie: Where is he? What could be keeping him?

R. Reader 1: That's all right, Maggie; your Mom and I will drive you down there.

Maggie: *Never!* I'd die of shame. Where *is* he?
(a long pause)

L. Reader 1: (calling to her husband) Honey, I think I just heard someone knocking on the door.

Maggie: I'll get it! I'll get it! I'll get it!
(suddenly perfectly composed) Oh, Hi, Jim. Want to go to that dance tonight?

R. Reader 1: You be back by eleven, you understand? No later.

L. Reader: How was the dance, Maggie?

Maggie: (aglow) Super!

**L. & R.
Reader 1:** Goodnight, dear.

Maggie: Goodnight.

(There is a pause to allow the mood to shift, then Maggie speaks)

Maggie: Dear God: It was wonderful to meet a person who will share his feelings with you, who appreciates so much being listened to. Thank you for Jim and the dance. (rote) Help me to be a good Christian. Help me to love you forever. Amen.

(There is a pause, then the action resumes at a brisk pace)

Maggie: Up in the morning; headache; homework not finished from the night before.

L. Reader 1:   Morning, Maggie.

Maggie: Humph!

R. Reader 1:   You look like you got up on the wrong side of the bed. Don't you have anything to wear but jeans?

Maggie: Off to school; headache; cloudy sky.

R. Reader 3:   Hi, Maggie.

Maggie: Hello.

R. Reader 3:   Got a smoke?

Maggie: Why don't you leave me alone, huh?

R. Reader 3:   What a pill!

L. Reader 2:   Now class, I would like to hear a stimulating question on the socio-economic triangle I have just explained. Maggie?

Maggie: Could you repeat the question, please?

L. Reader 1:   The fifth period will take place in the fourth period, except for girl's gym, which will not take place.

R. Reader 2:   (caustically) Little lady, what are you doing here in the hallway when class is supposed to be in session?

Maggie: I don't feel well. I've got a headache.

R. Reader 2:   Do you have a hall pass?

Maggie: Hello, Mom. This is Maggie. I got in trouble here at school this afternoon. Spoke back to the Dean of discipline. I wasn't feeling well and told him where to get off. Yes, Mom, I know, Mom. They want you down here right now to meet in conference with my counselor. (pause) Drive home with Mom. Head splitting. Mom's mad at me. Cloudy sky.

R. Reader 1: Maggie did *what?* What got into that daughter of yours?

L. Reader 1: Now she's suddenly *my* daughter!

R. Reader 1: Goodnight, Maggie.

Maggie: I'm sorry, Dad. It won't happen again.

L. Reader 1: 'Night, dear.

Maggie: Goodnight, Mom. Thanks for bailing me out at school.

(There is a pause to allow the mood to shift, then Maggie speaks)

Maggie: Dear God, I'm changing and at times like today I don't even recognize myself. I do want to grow and mature, but please leave me some of my old self, not only for tomorrow but next week and next year. Keep me faithful to you, help me to love you forever. Amen.

(There is a pause, then the action resumes at a brisk rate)

Maggie: Up in the morning; fog in the air; go to school.

R. Reader 3: Hello, my name is Ron.

Maggie: Uh, hello Ron.

R. Reader 3: Have you heard the Good News of Jesus?

Maggie: Uh, why ... yes. I'm a Catholic. A Catholic Christian.

R. Reader 3: But I want to know if you have truly accepted Christ as your personal Saviour.

Maggie: Well, as I said, I'm a Catholic, so I'm sure I have.

R. Reader 3: That doesn't answer my question: have you been baptized in the Spirit?

Maggie: Ron, I've even been confirmed.

R. Reader 3: Scripture says clearly that "unless ..."

Maggie: Please, why don't you just leave me alone? I'm not interested.

R. Reader 3:   (hurt) Uh ... OK ...

R. Reader 2:   Maggie, who was that you were just talking with?

Maggie: Oh, just some wierdo-kid.

L. Reader 3:   Class, I'd like to have some feedback on the film we have just watched together on *Sex and Society in the Psychedelic Age*. Maggie, would you like to begin?

Maggie: To tell the truth, I'm a little confused.

L. Reader 3:   In what way, *specifically*?

Maggie: Oh, nothing.

L. Reader 3:   No, no, please level with us. What didn't you like about the film?

Maggie: Well, I know this sounds kinda corny, but — (now Maggie is very serious) its treatment of sex seemed so ... so cosmetic and artificial. The movie didn't seem to think that sex had any connection with being a parent, having a home and a family. It treated sex more like a game than something important and ... sacred.

L. Reader 1:   Because it is a Monday, the fourth period driver's training class will not meet in the gym, but will ...

R. Reader 2:   Maggie, what a lot of hang-ups you have!

L. Reader 2:   I bet she still goes to church on Sunday.

L. Reader 3:   I think she's a Catholic or something like that.

L. Reader 1:   Fifth period students should report to the main parking lot at this time.

Maggie: Hi, Ron!

R. Reader 3:   Oh, hello. Did you think over what I said this morning?

Maggie:	Ron, I don't think I really need to be baptized again. But, could ask you a personal question?
R. Reader 3:	Sure.
Maggie:	Does it hurt when people make fun of your belief in Jesus?
R. Reader 3:	Of course it does. But if nothing's really important to you — how can you be important to yourself?
L. Reader 1:	How was school today, Maggie?
Maggie:	It was OK, Mom. The usual thing.
R. Reader 1:	I'm glad you like high school. For me those were the good ol' days!
Maggie:	Goodnight, Mom and Dad.
L. & R. **Reader 1:**	Goodnight.

(There is a pause to allow the mood to shift, then Maggie speaks)

Maggie:	Dear God, maybe some day I'll look back on school as the "good ol' days" too. But there is a lot of hurt involved along with the friends and fun ... and it's so very hard to stand up for what you believe when nobody else really cares. Dear God, help me to be a good Christian. Help me to love you forever. Amen.

(There is a pause, then the action resumes at a brisk pace)

Maggie:	Up in the morning and off to Church. Sun is shining; blossoms on the trees.
R. Reader 1:	How am I supposed to get into the parking lot with that fool driver blocking the entrance?
L. Reader 1:	Now, dear, remember it's Sunday.
R. Reader 3:	In the name of the Father and of the Son and of the Holy Spirit.
All:	Amen.
R. Reader 3:	In today's message, Our Lord reminds us ...

Maggie:	Dear Jesus, good morning. Thank you for coming into my heart in Communion, please help me ...
R. Reader 3:	Good morning, Maggie.
Maggie:	Good morning, Father Smith.
R. Reader 3:	Good morning, Mrs. White.
L. Reader 1:	'Morning, Father. Lovely day isn't it?
R. Reader 1:	What did you think of the sermon this morning, Maggie?
Maggie:	It was OK — but I didn't see hardly any of my friends.
L. Reader 1:	Maybe they were at the Saturday night Mass.
Maggie:	Sure, Mom. (Maggie turns on the tape recorder to noisy music again)
R. Reader 1:	Maggie, please turn off that noise. (Maggie does)
L. Reader 1:	Say, isn't that *Jim* walking up the street — the boy who took you to the Spring dance last year?
R. Reader 1:	Yes it is. He was such a polite, clean-cut young man.
Maggie:	Oh, Dad, he was *so immature.* The only person he could ever talk about was himself.
R. Reader 1:	Now when I was young, before I started working at the office ...
Maggie:	Good night, Dad.
R. Reader 1:	Don't let the bed bugs bite.
Maggie:	Good night, Mom.
L. Reader:	Good night, Maggie.
	(There is a pause, then the final sequence begins)
Maggie:	Dear God, it just goes on and on. Up in the morning, off to school, clouds in the sky.
L. Reader 2:	Maggie, Judy got busted last night for smoking pot.

R. Reader: Maggie, I really like your new hair style.

Maggie: My life seems to always be changing yet somehow remains the same.

L. Reader 3:   Little girl, thank you for helping me across this busy street.

R. Reader 1:   There was this fight on the second floor, this kid was being stomped on!

R. Reader 3:   Maggie, this particular essay is simply magnificent. It couldn't be more perfect.

Maggie: (slowly and clearly, pausing between phrases) Growing up is such a funny thing.

L. Reader 1:   Doesn't my daughter own anything but jeans?

Maggie: The more I study, the taller I get; things seem to break up into more and more pieces that won't go back together again.

R. Reader 3:   Got a smoke?

Maggie: And yet underneath there is something good and pure about this pain; a sense that I can help other people bear with their own problems; a hope that somehow there is meaning to it all.

R. Reader 2:   Where did you get those hang-ups?

L. Reader 3:   Who's that I saw you with yesterday during the ten minute break?

R. Reader 2:   That's a cute dress you've got on.

L. Reader 1:   Maggie, your grandmother died suddenly this morning.

R. Reader 3:   Stop staring out the window and pay attention to class.

Maggie: Oh, God, help me to grow into what you intended me to be. Help me to share your love, truth, goodness with others tomorrow, next week, and next year.

R. Reader 2:   What answer did you get for number 9?
R. Reader 3:   This is absolutely the best essay I've seen all year.
R. Reader 1:   When I was young, before I started working...
Maggie: Goodnight, Mom.
L. Reader 1:   Goodnight, Maggie.
Maggie: 'Night, Dad.
R. Reader 1:   Goodnight Maggie. Don't let the bed bugs bite!
                         The end.

APPENDIX
Learning from Parish History

The faith journey of any parish community is a rich source of inspiration for young and old alike. How this story is told, and its contents, will of course vary. Roots and Redwoods *appended here tells of the early days of Our Lady of Mount Carmel Parish in Mill Valley, California. It is given here as a model for a simple dramatic presentation and an inducement to others to set down their own unique histories. The dramatic reading has been given annually in small group settings since 1976 by the Junior High students of our Religious Education Program.*

ROOTS AND REDWOODS: The Early History of Our Lady of Mount Carmel Parish, Mill Valley, California

Note: The following script is and is not a drama. There are no real scenes in which dialogue is exchanged between characters. At the same time, you should give the impression that you are a real person, someone who lived through the events narrated and is now sharing them with the audience. It is suggested that you use a cane, wear a hat, or do something by the way of costume to help you act out your role.

Narrator: (said in a normal manner, not as an old person) Mount Carmel Church is people before it is a building. It is God's presence among these people, before it is their presence before him. And though we reverence the past, if the presence of Christ in our words and actions is not vigorous in our community and homes today, then the underlying meaning of all those who have gone before us in faith has been lost. But though the past cannot replace the present, it can strengthen it. Our heritage can show us our roots and be a source of inspiration.

Reader #1: *Roots* you say? *City* of Mill Valley? Pshaw! If you leave out the old mill that Irishman John Reed put in the creek here back when these hills were still a part of Mexico, there wasn't a town here — barely a house — until 1890. Now this is not to say there weren't people — of course there were! But this was ranch country. The hills were more weeds than trees, and outside of the Portugese dairymen supplying San Francisco with milk, and the Portugese fishermen sailing out of Sausalito, there was more *nothing* here than *something!* Roots you say? We had them for sure; but they were pretty short and tender back in 1890. You ask me about the church, sonny? The fact is that Catholics were neither all that common nor all that popular back then. We always seemed just a little bit slower and worse off than Catholics in other parts of California. Take the Mission in San Rafael, for example. It was the second to last of the 21 California missions, not built until 1817. By the time of the Gold Rush in 1849, it had been closed and abandoned. For more than half of the last century there wasn't a single Catholic priest in Marin County, that's how well off we were!

Reader #2: Oh, landsakes yes, the roots were tender and young in 1890. After the mission in San Rafael closed, the Catholic Church here just had to start again from scratch — and for that we can thank the Portugese immigrants, whose pestering finally convinced the first bishop of San Francisco, a Dominican from Spain by the name of Joseph Alemany, to give them a church in Sausalito in 1881.

They named the Sausalito Church "Star of the Sea" in honor of Mary — and what a parish it was! It included Bolinas, San Rafael, Tiburon, and our little valley here. If you wanted to go to church on Sunday, you went by foot, horse, or wagon over the hills to the little fishing village of Sausalito. That's our roots in a neat bundle: one church and a whole empty county. But things were about to happen. The people and a very special priest were coming.

Reader #3:   Who really gets the credit for our church? It's hard to say, so many people played a part. But one thing is for sure: this might still be a pasture if there hadn't been a rush of folks here in the 1880s and '90s, and for this we gotta give the *trees* the credit! Kinda fitting that this Church is trimmed in redwood, because it was the trees that attracted the city people here from San Francisco, back in the 1890s. Oh, there were other things. The streams were full of fish, the mountain was there for hiking, and a new railroad line had just been run up here from the ferry dock in Sausalito.

But I *still* say it was the redwood trees that gave this valley its reputation in those days as the finest picnic spot anywhere around San Francisco. The kids could rent a donkey from a fancy new stable called Dowds, then ride up the pasture along the old Mill Creek. Older folks could stay at the posh Blithedale Hotel, which used to be up the canyon a few blocks from here: the creek had been dammed off to make a big pond, and you could rent a rowboat — or play tennis instead, if you preferred. If you couldn't afford the Blithdale, you could try one of the others: the Eastern, the Abbey, the Madrona, or the Kennilworth.

As for homes, well yes, there were a few big private houses here and there, as well as a good number of small summer cottages. But most visitors who

came for the summer just lived in tents set up on
wooden platforms.

That was the way things were in the year 1890,
when a land auction was held by the Tamalpais
Land and Water Company. And with that auction
of what is today all the downtown section of Mill
Valley, it at last began to look as if there might be a
real city here someday. In fact, down in Sausalito
the Catholic pastor began to wonder if maybe it
wasn't time to start thinking about putting up
some kind of church in Mill Valley.

Reader #4:   1893, by Jingo! That was a year. A Democratic
lawyer from New York, name of Grover
Cleveland, was elected President; six million acres
of Oklahoma land opened up and settled in a single
day, a World's Fair in Chicago and a stock market
crash — all at the same time. I guess not many
people sat up and took notice when a certain
Catholic pastor in Sausalito by the name of Father
John Valentini talked Bishop Riordon into giving
this valley a mission church just like he had for
Bolinas and Tiburon a few years earlier. Since Fr.
Valentini was still the only priest in Southern
Marin, it all just meant more work for him, driving
his horse and two-wheeled cart on the old dirt
roads one Sunday, the 15 miles up to Bolinas,
another out to the mission at Tiburon, and once
each month to us.

Fr. Valentini had always been the traveling kind.
He started from the town of Como in the lake
country of northern Italy and then went down to
the Foreign Missionary Seminary in Milan. When
ordained a priest in the 1850's, he sailed off for
Hong Kong, China, where he was in charge of a
mission school. Finally, in 1863 he came to work as
a missionary in California. He was an intelligent
man, could speak Italian, French, German,
Spanish, Portugese, and English. And he was a

born missionary. "No Church? Well, Mr. Thompson, you have the biggest front room of anyone I know, let's have Mass at your place!" Mr. James Thompson was a San Francisco bank teller who'd built himself a home here for his wife and six children two years earlier. It was in his house at 620 Molino Avenue that the first Mass was ever said in Mill Valley, with two of his young sons being the servers.

But it wasn't big enough and shortly afterwards we moved into a new one room grammar school that had just been built on Summit. Our first permanent Church? That was a ways off yet, but we did have a little plot of land that the Tamalpais Land and Water Company gave us, when they were also setting aside pieces for the Episcopal and Congregational Churches. And having a piece of land, Father Valentini gave us a name: Our Lady of Mount Carmel.

You may wonder where the name came from. I said that Father Valentini was a traveling man. Now in Palestine overlooking the bay at Haifa is the first church ever built in honor of Our Lady. It's on a mountain, Mount Carmel, and some think that Fr. Valentini's ship put in there on his way to China many years before. Be that as it may, when it came time to choose a name, Fr. Valentini decided that the church that would go up on our empty hillside plot overlooking the bay should be called Our Lady of Mount Carmel.

Reader #5: Let me tell you, a parish church is the crossing point of the most trivial human doings and the sacred holiness of God. Its history is a cycle of births, deaths, and celebrations, which because they are ends in themselves, leave a few .races. Take our first ten years, for example: Mass went on in the Thompson home at least into 1894. Then the Sunday community moved to

Summit School, a big one-room school house that
had opened with 35 students the previous year on
the hillside up behind where Old Mill School is
today. On Sundays when it rained hard, the usually
muddy Miller Avenue would go completely under
water and Fr. Valentini's cart wouldn't make it in.
During January and February of 1895, this happened four times. Mass, of course, was celebrated
in Latin. But the sermons were given first to all
those sitting on the right side of the hall in the
Portugese language, and then to all those on the
left side in English. On Christmas and *big* occasions, Fr. Valentini would add a third talk in
Italian, just for good measure.

From those earliest years, a fund-raising concert
and dance were held each summer. In 1896 we
filled a hall full of town's people and summer
guests and raised a whopping $165.00. You can
imagine how happy this made us feel, especially
since even the Christmas collection at the time
wasn't averaging more than $10.00.

At last in 1898, five years after Our Lady of Mount
Carmel Parish began, our new church was ready
for dedication. Wasn't the biggest building on
earth — about forty feet wide and fifty feet long —
but it was our own, and with the stained glass
window behind the altar of Our Lady of Mount
Carmel, which had been donated by the Deffeback
family, it was something we could be proud of.
Archbishop William Riordon came over on the
ferry from San Francisco in October to do the
blessing. Strange, what people remember.

The bishop spent the night at the Thompson home,
on the hill behind the Old Mill, and the next
morning during the ceremony gave the parish a
chalice and a paten as gifts. That's about all we
know, except one thing: good Mrs. Thompson kept

a copy of what she had served the bishop at supper — and his reaction to it. Interesting reading, I think. They had red clam soup, white fish with oyster sauce. Archbishop said he never ate fish. Then there was roast beef (the Archbishop liked the gravy), scalloped potatoes, string bean salad, apple custard pie, gelatin, cake, and coffee. He ate all this, but only sipped the coffee.

Reader #6: So the parish was born and blessed. But there was a sad ending to the first chapter of its life. On July 22 of the following year, the annual summer benefit for Fr. Valentini was held at Landgraff's Villa. Some of the Thompson kids helped that evening at the lemonade stand, and Mrs. Thompson sold home-sewn items at the fancy work table. Four months later Mrs. Thompson died suddenly. Before the year was out, her husband died as well. The six orphaned children, resolving to stay together at all costs, left their Mill Valley home and returned to San Francisco.

Reader #7: For the next 8 years, things stayed about the same. I've got some old clippings here from a newspaper called the *Record Enterprise* from those days. They bring back memories of moments happy and sad. Maybe I could share them with you:
The Record Enterprise, June 21, 1907
"ARCHBISHOP PAYS VISIT TO VALLEY, UNCLE OF KING OF PORTUGAL CONFIRMS LARGE CLASS OF CHILDREN HERE"
Last Sunday was a gala day at the Catholic Church of Our Lady of Mount Carmel in Mill Valley. Archbishop Di Silva of Lisbon, an uncle of the King of Portugal, who has been spending some time in this country at the request of the Pope looking after Catholic interests and especially those of his compatriots, was received at the depot on his descent from Mount Tamalpais where he spent the night. The sacred edifice was crowded, many being unable to even enter the building. The Archbishop said Mass and a full choir with

orchestral accompaniment rendered music proper for the occasion. After Mass the Archbishop administered confirmation to a large class of children and grown persons, having previously given the children their first holy communion. He then preached in English a very entertaining sermon appropriate to the occasion. After the services were over he was entertained at breakfast by Mr. & Mrs. O'Shaughnessey and later left for Sausalito where he was given an elaborate reception.

Reader #8: *The Record Enterprise*, July 5, 1907
"CATHOLIC CHURCH TO GIVE MOONLIGHT GARDEN PARTY"
A pleasant time may be looked forward to on the afternoon and evening of July 27, when a Moonlight Garden Party and Dance will be given on the pretty grounds of the Outdoor Art Club in aid of the building fund of Our Lady of Mount Carmel Church. Those in charge of the affair are making elaborate preparations. During the afternoon program children will be admitted to the grounds without charge. Several pretty features for the benefit of the youngsters have been arranged."
The Record Enterprise, August 2, 1907
... the raffles of the gold watch, the "Teddy Bear" and the sofa pillow were highly interesting and provided excellent sources of revenue for the fete. A ... musical program was rendered in the early part of the evening and at its conclusion dancing was indulged in until a late hour. The following numbers made up the program:
1. Selections by Hyne's Orchestra
2. Vocal solo, Miss Anita C. Gleason, assisted by Miss Edith Gowan
3. Chinese Stunt, Mr. Harry Sheldon and Bob McMahon
4. Violin Solo ...
5. Soprano Solo, Miss Mabel Kearney ... accompaniment by Miss Amy Breen

Reader #9:   The earthquake of 1906 had at least one good result, if you ask me: the new folk who moved into town finally made it possible for us to have a full time priest of our own. The year was 1908, and his name was Fr. Joseph Sesnon. In some ways he was a local boy. Though he had been raised in San Francisco, the son of a wealthy importer, he had spent a good number of his summer vacations while he was growing up right here in our own valley. Fr. Sesnon was something special. In the 1890's he had graduated from the University of Santa Clara, and then had gone to Paris, France, to study opera. Then at the age of 30, he decided his true calling was to be a priest, and so he went off to Rome and signed up at the famous Gregorian University where four years later he was ordained. He first came to live in Mill Valley from Sausalito (where he had been Fr. Valentini's assistant) in 1908, even though Fr. Valentini continued to keep the title of pastor. Fr. Sesnon always amazed people with his beautiful singing voice, both at solemn church services and at the summer benefits in the Outdoor Art Club across the street from where we are tonight. He taught catechism to the children's choir — not an easy thing since there were so few young people around.

Reader #10:   We were still a small community in Fr. Sesnon's days, averaging about twenty baptisms and five or six weddings a year. Yet even at that size we were getting too big for our little Church. Two plots of land were bought; one piece on the corner of Carmelita and East Blithedale, the other at Buena Vista and East Blithedale, where we are today. The beginning of 1916 was the start of a new era, with work beginning on a new $30,000 church and rectory. But it also marks the end of Mount Carmel's pioneer days.

You see: Fr. Sesnon had not only a good singing voice, but he was also an outstanding speaker. Soon after 1916 began, Archbishop Hanna of San Francisco announced that Fr. Sesnon had been

chosen to teach Sacred Eloquence at the Catholic
University in Washington, D.C. Then a short time
later, on the afternoon of April 8, good old Fr.
Valentini passed away. (Pause)
What's left from those old times that might help us
remember them? One thing above all, Fr. Sesnon's
statue of the crucified saviour, the body of Christ,
which Fr. Sesnon bought for the parish, hangs over
the altar of worship in our church today, as it has
stood over the celebration of God's Word and
Bread now for more than sixty years. I can think of
no more fitting reminder of the love, effort, joy,
and sadness which Christ's presence has inspired
and blessed down through the years in the life of
the Catholic community of Mill Valley, California.

Dramas and Dramatic Resources...

How the Word Became Flesh by Michael E. Moynahan, SJ
ISBN 0-89390-029-X
Simple-to-use story dramas, with complete staging instructions, for use in church with adults or in school with young adults **$10.95**

Angels to Wish By by Joseph J. Juknialis
ISBN 0-89390-051-6
Story prayers for church and classroom **$7.95**

The Stick Stories by Margie Brown
ISBN 0-89390-035-4
Biblical character sketches that lend fresh insight into the scriptures **$6.95**

Plays to Play With in Class by Sally-Anne Milgrim
ISBN 0-89390-060-5
Eight one-act scripts with accompanying language arts activities **$10.95**

Playwriting Step-By-Step by Marsh Cassady
ISBN 0-89390-056-7
Thorough, practical guidebook for beginning playwrights, with organizational suggestions and marketing hints **8.95**

Some Trust in Chariots by Donald Eidson
ISBN 0-89390-055-9
Historical drama about Enoch Mather Marvin, the first Methodist bishop in the Missouri Conference **$9.95**

Actions, Gestures, & Bodily Attitudes by Carolyn Deitering
ISBN 0-89390-021-4
Examines basic Christian ritual actions and bodily movements as prayer forms **$10.95**

See your local dealer for these and other resources and aids for Christian worship, or write:

Resource Publications, Inc.
160 E. Virginia Street
San Jose, CA 95112